PHOTO JOLTS!

IMAGE-BASED ACTIVITIES THAT INCREASE CLARITY, CREATIVITY, AND CONVERSATION

BY GLENN HUGHES &
SIVASAILAM 'THIAGI' THIAGARAJAN

Find us on the web at *SMARTasHell.com, PhotoJolts.com*, or *Thiagi.com*.

To report errors, please send a note to *info@smartashell.com*.

ISBN: 978-0-9894655-1-9
LCCN: 2013912220
Oct 10, 2013

For information on getting permission for reprints and excerpts, contact *info@smartashell.com*.

SAH PUBLISHING
Santa Clara, California, USA

ACKNOWLEDGMENTS

Glenn thanks:

- *Angie Elschlager*: For her constant enthusiasm and eternal patience.
- *Sam Hughes*: Because that's a damn fine tree to fall from.
- *Brent Bloom, Ken Wells, and the rest of my colleagues in KLA-Tencor's Corporate Learning Center*: For making what we do impossible to call work.
- *My teachers*: Known as participants in most organizations, I learn more from these folks than I could ever teach them.
- *Kevin Small*: For the two hours of insights that will last me a lifetime.
- *Nancy Duarte and Cal Wick:* For the friendship, mentorship, and leadership they've provided to me and countless others.
- *Jeff Miller*: For the cover photography.
- *Tram Nguyen*: For the cover design contributions.

Thiagi thanks:

- *Regina Rowland and Tracy Tagliati*: The people who tried unsuccessfully to transform me into a visual thinker.
- *Lucy Thiagarajan*: The person who unsuccessfully tried to get me to clean my desk.
- *Harold Stolovitch and Bob Mager*: The people who tried to get me to speak American English.
- *Matthew Richter*: The person who unsuccessfully tried to increase my business acumen.
- *You*: The thousands of people around the world who read what I write and attend my training sessions in spite of my funny accent, visual illiteracy, and cluttered desk.
- *The wonderful cooks*: Those around the world who create spicy South Indian vegetarian cuisine without which I cannot write and speak.

CONTENTS

FIND SUPPLEMENTAL VIDEOS,
WORKSHEETS, AND LINKS AT:

HTTP://SMARTASHELL.COM/BLOG/PJRESOURCES

OBJECTIVES

After completing *Photo Jolts!* the reader will be able to select, facilitate, and debrief activities that increase clarity, creativity, and conversation in any individual, team, or organization.

PART ONE

At the end of Part One, the reader will be able to:

- Define a Photo Jolt
- Define six reasons for using a Photo Jolt activity
- Choose appropriate images for a Photo Jolt activity
- Identify the factors that determine an effective Photo Jolt activity

PART TWO

At the end of Part Two, the reader will be able to:

- Identify an appropriate Photo Jolt for their purpose, topic, time, and audience
- Prepare the appropriate resources for a selected Photo Jolt activity
- Run a selected Photo Jolt activity, using the prepared flow
- Modify a selected Photo Jolt, using the proposed variations
- Debrief a selected Photo Jolt, using the debrief questions

PART THREE

At the end of Part Three, the reader will be able to:

- Customize a Photo Jolt, using more than 25 suggested modifications
- Create a new Photo Jolt, using the Photo Jolts template
- Assess images, using the Image Scorecard
- Assess a Photo Jolt activity, using the Activity Scorecard

x

FOREWORD

Images are powerful. While you might not remember a full sentence from a recent book, you can probably summon an image of Neil Armstrong's moonwalk, the horror of New York City's Twin Towers tragedy, or a faded photograph of your parents in their youth.

Unfortunately, the power of images is underutilized. While words are beautiful, they are not the only way to communicate in training and presentations.

A little known creative device is to use pictures as a tool to generate memorable communications. Emotive images can bring consensus and spark creativity in unexpected directions.

I've spent more than 25 years of my life helping people harness the power of images to change the world through their slides. With my books *Slide:ology* and *Resonate*, I've worked to help corporations, non-profits, and individuals transform their words into images, their images into stories, their stories into actions, and their actions into positive change. I've seen the transformative effect of images as they amplify a message, change minds and become the flashpoint for a movement.

I'm not alone in the visual movement. In *Brain Rules,* John Medina explains how we learn and remember best through pictures. In *Back of the Napkin*, Dan Roam demonstrates a process for "solving problems and selling ideas" through sketches. In *Visual Thinking* and *Visual Meetings*, David Sibbett shares how to facilitate group processes with large graphics. In *Gamestorming*, Dave Gray, Sunni Brown, and James Macanufo show how combining games and visuals can transform organizations.

Each of those books has been a game-changer that I devoured and kept on my bookshelf, and so is *Photo Jolts!*

Like those books, *Photo Jolts!* is clear and actionable. Glenn and Thiagi show us how to use images to create positive change in individuals, teams, and organizations. *Photo Jolts!* uses images to destroy barriers to communication.

I experienced my first Photo Jolt with my friend and colleague, *Presentation Zen* author Garr Reynolds. Glenn asked each of us to choose an image that demonstrated what we admire about the other. I chose a cherry blossom image that I felt captured Garr's gift of simplicity. Garr chose a candle that represented the light of inspiration and warmth that he sees in my work. I found the activity engaging and enlightening. It was fun - and the visuals provoked a deeper response than words alone. Garr and I identified a 'fire and ice' relationship that we would not have discovered verbally.

When I heard that Glenn and Thiagi had written this book documenting photo facilitation techniques, I was not surprised. If I was asked to handpick two people on this planet to write an activity book that shows us how to use images for learning, these are the guys.

I met Glenn Hughes in 2008, shortly after the release of my first book *Slide:ology*. Passionate about the concepts, he came alongside me like a big brother and helped me transform our training program into a masterwork. He's a remarkable facilitator, photographer, and communicator. Thiagi, meanwhile, is a legend in the training industry. He is a prolific writer, an in-demand speaker, and an influential training designer.

Together, Glenn and Thiagi deliver on the promise of the book's subtitle, "Image-based Activities that Increase Clarity, Creativity, and Conversation." The recipe format is clear and easy to follow. The 51 activities provide more than 300 variations, 21 topic areas, hundreds of debrief questions, and 27 ways to modify any exercise. And, while this is a 'how-to' book, they maintain a conversational tone throughout.

It's true that images are underutilized for reflection and learning purposes today. With *Photo Jolts!* in your hand, however, that will change. So, grab a handful of photos, postcards, or magazine images. Gather your friends, family, or colleagues. Open this book and experience *Photo Jolts!*

Nancy Duarte

CEO, Duarte, Inc

Author, *Slide:ology, Resonate, HBR Guide to Persuasive Presentations*

Sunnyvale, California

Nancy Duarte and Garr Reynolds play Photo Jolts!
http://YouTube.com/SMARTasHellVideo

PART ONE

ABOUT PHOTO JOLTS!

AN INTRODUCTION TO PHOTO JOLTS!

Welcome to Photo Jolts!

WHAT IS PHOTO JOLTS ABOUT?

Photo Jolts! is a cookbook. It contains fifty-one recipes for stimulating clarity, creativity, and conversation in individuals, pairs, or groups. The main ingredient is the intentionally provocative use of photographs.

WHY DID WE WRITE THIS BOOK?

While the use of photographs for learning – often called photo facilitation – has existed for decades, we wrote this book for the simplest and most obvious reason; it didn't already exist. Now it does.

We've been familiar with photo facilitation for a long time and had mixed experiences with it. We've seen it done with powerful images; we've seen it done with weak images. We've seen it dispensed as a quick activity with no depth; we've seen it extended beyond its useful length. We've seen it debriefed masterfully; we've seen it debriefed poorly or not at all. We've seen it implemented trivially; we've seen it implemented with great effect. Increasingly, we've used it in ways that facilitated breakthroughs for individuals and teams.

In 2012, we were attending the American Society for Training and Development's annual conference in Denver, Colorado. While playing with a deck of *Photo Jolts!* cards, we started trading ideas. One of us showed the other an activity. The other countered with a different game. This continued for three days, until one of us said, "We should publish these."

Over the next twelve months, we created more than 150 Photo Jolt activities with over 500 variations. We filmed seven *Photo Jolts!* videos in Chicago. We tested the activities in coaching, in workshops, and at conferences. The 51 *Photo Jolts!* and more than 300 variations that you'll find in this pages have been used successfully with audiences around the world – including the United States, Switzerland, Singapore, Malaysia, India, Korea, and Australia.

WHO ARE WE?

We're the guys on the cover of this book. We've accumulated years of experience helping individuals and teams improve their performance. We've published books, designed games and workshops, worked with big companies, and won multiple awards for our work. Look us up on our respective websites – *SMARTasHell.com* and *Thiagi.com* - or on LinkedIn to see what we've done lately. Feel free to drop us a note and join our networks to start or continue a conversation.

WHO SHOULD READ THIS BOOK?

If you are interested in increasing clarity, creativity, or conversation with yourself, your family, your students, your team, or your organization, you should read – and use – *Photo Jolts!*

The target audience for this book includes:

- ✓ Trainers
- ✓ Facilitators
- ✓ Human Resource Professionals
- ✓ Teachers
- ✓ Coaches
- ✓ Therapists
- ✓ Counselors
- ✓ Managers
- ✓ Team Leaders
- ✓ Global Teams
- ✓ Couples
- ✓ Parents
- ✓ Individuals

WHAT DO I NEED TO KNOW TO RUN A PHOTO JOLT?

This book contains an activity called *Kipling's Questions* (pg 255). It was inspired by the words of author Rudyard Kipling:

> *I keep six honest serving men,*
> *They taught me all I knew;*
> *Their names are what and why and when,*
> *And how and where and who.*

Here are our answers to Kipling's six questions, as they pertain to *Photo Jolts!*

WHAT IS A PHOTO JOLT?

A *Photo Jolt!* is an image-based activity that increases clarity, creativity, and conversation. *Photo Jolts!* work with individuals or teams; at home, at school, or in the workplace. There are two components to *Photo Jolts!* - the images and the activities.

The Images

The best images for a *Photo Jolts!* activity meet seven criteria:

1. **High resolution**: The best images are clear and easy to view. No pixilation. No fingerprints. No grease stains. No folds. No squinting to see what's in the picture.
2. **High impact**: The best images grab the attention of busy, distracted participants.
3. **Immersive**: Simple or complex, an effective Photo Jolt image invites exploration. The image should stand up to at least five to ten seconds of viewing.

4. *Ambiguous*: The perfect image can be interpreted positively and negatively. It should not include text that influences the viewer.

5. *Varied*: Facilitating a variety of responses requires a variety of images. The ideal deck has a mix of subjects: animals, nature, architecture, food, people, and objects. There is a range of emotional content representing beauty, ugliness, safety, danger, joy, hate, life, and death. The deck has a wide palette of colors and there is a range of masculine and feminine content.

6. *Global*: The best set of images includes familiar and unfamiliar content. A global set of images from a range of countries and cultures allows every participant to experience surprise without feeling excluded.

7. *Sturdy*: Participants handle these images frequently and with great energy. The image set must hold up to use and reuse.

The images in this book are representative of strong *Photo Jolts!* images. They are high resolution and high impact. They are immersive. Most importantly, they are ambiguous. Look at the photo on page 2. What does it represent to you?

One person might say the image represents power. Another person might say that it represents excessive authority. A third might say that it represents tradition. This range of responses is critical to creating powerful *Photo Jolts!* results.

A strong set of images is not created by accident. It is assembled through extensive testing in hundreds of sessions, with thousands of participants around the world. The best image sets are optimized to drive deep thought and powerful discussions.

The Activities (or 'Jolts')

The second component of a *Photo Jolt!* is the activity. The term 'Jolt' refers to the following conditions:

- A 'Jolt' is a short activity or experience that provokes a participant into a new state of awareness or attitude about a topic, situation, or human being.

- A 'Jolt' is an activity that is run in as little as one minute and then is debriefed for up to one hour.

- A 'Jolt' inspires conversation. While it may precede or follow a lecture, a lecture is not a 'Jolt'.

The most basic *Photo Jolt!* is one we call *A Thousand Words* (pg. 37) because a picture is said to be worth a thousand words.

This activity – which is a great icebreaker, party game, or introduction to a meeting or training – asks participants to choose a photographic metaphor for their topic or challenge. For example, I might ask you to choose a metaphor for your career. The participants then share their photos and explain the metaphor.

You'll find four examples of this activity - with authors Rick Gilbert, Robert H. Thompson, Dan Madison, and Ed Muzio - at *http://YouTube.com/SMARTasHellVideo*.

WHY USE PHOTO JOLTS?

There are six reasons to use *Photo Jolts!*

1. *A team or individual is lacking clarity.*

   Photo Jolts! activities help teams build a common visual language around a topic, an issue, or a challenge. I can talk about the chaos in my customer situation or I can show you a picture of statues with their heads cut off. Which is more powerful? By the way, in many cases, it's the search for the image that creates clarity for the user. This is a powerful tool in one-on-one coaching.

2. **You or your team is lacking _creativity_.**

   If you or your team is stuck for new ideas or solutions, a *Photo Jolts!* activity can kick-start innovation.

   One example is called *Risk Assessment* (pg. 217). Choose a random photograph and ask, "How does this image suggest a risk," and then choose another random photograph and ask, "What solution does this suggest?"

   Another example is *And Then...* (pg. 269), where participants practice improvisation by using random cards to build stories.

3. **You need to drive _conversation_.**

   Photo Jolts! create dialog at meetings, parties, or training sessions. People find it much easier to talk about an image than to talk about their feelings. While I might not say that I'm frustrated, I might choose an image that illustrates the barriers I'm facing.

   We also use *Photo Jolts!* to drive learning conversations. Trainers love to lecture about leadership, but it's far more engaging to have twenty managers choose cards that represent leadership and then have them share and discuss their ideas.

4. **You want to create _engagement_.**

   Photo Jolts! are engaging. They are hands-on, so they create a kinesthetic experience; they are visually stimulating; and the activities create a sense of surprise as participants try to guess what an image means to someone else.

   A standard icebreaker activity asks participants to introduce themselves by stating their name, company, and job. Facilitators attempt to spice this up by asking participants to share a favorite holiday spot or a detail that no one knows about you. Yawn... During these introductions, no one is listening. Each person is thinking about what he or she will say next. It's not effective.

Contrast that with a *Photo Jolts!* icebreaker, where participants choose an image that represents their job. Now, as each participant shares their image, the other participants lean in to see the photo and guess the metaphor. Each person listens intently to the speaker. If the metaphor matches what the listener was thinking, a common ground has been established. If the metaphor is different, the listener is surprised, often laughing or learning a new perspective. Either way, we've created engagement.

5. *You're working with <u>mixed audiences.</u>*

   Photo Jolts! need no reading skills, no specialized knowledge, no complex rules. They work with any culture, any language, any industry, and any age group.

   When we facilitate these activities around the world, we set up the exercise in English and then let the participants finish the activity in their native languages. *Photo Jolts!* are truly 'one size fits all'.

6. *You don't have a big <u>budget.</u>*

   Photo Jolts! are an inexpensive activity for coaches, facilitators, trainers, and managers. One deck returns hundreds of hours of high-impact conversations at a fraction of the cost of a high-priced offsite or engagement.

WHERE DO I FIND PHOTO JOLTS IMAGES?

A facilitator seeking *Photo Jolts!* images has two options: make or buy.

Make

It's said that photo facilitation started as a 'do-it-yourself' project when a facilitator used a bundle of personal postcards to stimulate conversation. When it worked, word spread, and other facilitators used postcards or tore images from magazines to create collections. Still others sorted through their own photographs to build a deck.

Any of these methods can work, if you're willing and able to create a high-quality deck with a variety of subjects and appropriate complexity.

Buy

Fortunately, for those who don't want to build their own decks, there are companies that sell image-based card decks. In this book, we refer to our *Photo Jolts!* decks (*http://PhotoJolts.com*). These cards come in two sizes:

- *Poker size*: This is a pack of 54 poker-quality cards. It's affordable, easy to carry, and easy to use. It offers a mix of images that's global in nature.
- *Postcard size*: This pack of 88 cards is great for showing your images in larger groups.

The *Photo Jolts!* line also includes a number of specialty decks:

- *People Jolts!* This pack features 54 images of people. It's great for customer service workshops, persona testing, and emotional intelligence discussions.
- *Animal Jolts!* This pack features 54 images of animals. Animals provide abundant metaphors. Think 'busy as a bee' or 'clever like a fox'.

- *Food Jolts!* This pack features 54 images of food. 'Hot', 'spicy', 'raw', disgusting', 'bountiful' – food engages our minds and our eyes.

- *ArchiJolts!* This pack features 54 images of architecture. The range of cultures, eras, materials, and styles is rich in metaphorical content.

- *Photo Provocations.* This deck includes 54 questions that you can ask about your *Photo Jolts!* images. You can use these to prepare for a session, to generate random questions in a session, or to let large groups facilitate their own discussions.

- *Poker Jolts!* This poker deck offers a facilitator the means to sort participants by color, suit, or number. You can also play card games when you're not running an activity.

The *Photo Jolts!* line is not your only option. Alternative sources for image sets are listed on page 354. Remember - the activities in this book work with any photos you decide to use.

HOW MANY IMAGES OR DECKS DO I NEED?

Our experience with thousands of participants shows that the ideal number of cards per player is 4-to-1. In other words, a deck of 54 cards is perfect for 12 or 13 players. If you use fewer cards, participants feel that their options are limited. If you use more cards, participants can feel 'paralyzed by choice' and struggle to choose a card. So, for example, if you run an activity for 24 people, your best option is to use two decks - but don't let a limited number of cards stop you from running an activity. These numbers are just guidelines.

HOW DO I CHOOSE A PHOTO JOLTS! ACTIVITY?

We ask six questions when choosing or creating a *Photo Jolts!* activity.

1. *What is my topic or challenge?*

    Is it customer service, a new product, career choices, a relationship, or the civil war? You must define the topic or challenge.

2. *Am I increasing clarity, creativity, or conversation?*

    Knowing this helps you run and debrief the activity. If we are looking for clarity, we won't stop until we reach it. If we're looking for creativity, we'll set a target number of ideas. If we're looking for conversation, we'll aim to provoke a continuing, deeper dialog.

3. *Will I ask participants to choose a photo, or will I give them a random image?*

    If we want participants to express themselves, we ask them to choose the photo. If, on the other hand, we're trying to stretch their perspective, we'll give them a random photo.

4. *What format will I use?*

    Is this a competition with rules? Are we working as teams? Or are we sharing as individuals?

5. *Will we share our results as a large group, as small groups, or as pairs?*

    This largely depends on time considerations.

6. *How will I debrief the exercise?*

    Will we focus on common themes raised in the room? Will we focus on differences? Will we have the group consolidate their results? Will we use these comments as a bridge to another activity or will we focus on assigning action steps?

WHEN & WHERE CAN I USE PHOTO JOLTS?

A great advantage of *Photo Jolts!* is that they work anywhere. We've used them in meeting rooms, offices, classrooms, bars, restaurants, on the beach, on airplanes, and standing up in a conference hall. Some *Photo Jolts!* require a pencil and paper or perhaps a desk or table, but most just require an active mind.

ADDITIONAL TIPS

- *Audience.* Don't let anyone tell you "These won't work with my audience." *Photo Jolts!* work with anyone from infants to executives (yes, there is a slim but distinct difference).

- *Time.* Limit participants to one or two minutes to choose an image. More time doesn't seem to help the people who have difficulty choosing.

- *Cards.* Try to adhere to our '4-to-1' guideline. Set out four photo images per participant. Ten participants equal forty images. Fewer images leave participants feeling like they didn't have sufficient choice; more images induce paralysis through choice.

- *Observe.* Observe how participants engage in the act of choosing their images. From our experience, 25% of participants have an image in their head and then search for it; 65% are looking for a photo that inspires them to think of a metaphor; 10% don't care what image they get. Ask and discover how your participants make their choices. Also note 'hoarders' – those who grab a bunch of images, and 'perfectionists' – those who keep looking for the perfect image and then still aren't happy.

HOW SHOULD I USE THIS BOOK?

1. *Download* the *Photo Jolts!* pdf supplement from *http://PhotoJolts.com*. This document includes six full-color reference photos, every worksheet in this book, and a blank *Photo Jolts!* Template.

2. *Watch* our videos at *http://YouTube.com/SMARTasHellVideo* for examples, instructions, and inspiration.

3. *Review* *How to Read Photo Jolts* (pg. 17) to understand our recipe format.

4. *Run* one of the 51 Photo Jolt recipes that make up the bulk of this book.

5. *Read* *Modifying a Photo Jolt* (pg. 345) to customize an activity for your situation.

6. *Use* the *Photo Jolt Template* (pg. 348) to create new activities. Send your ideas to *info@SMARTasHell.com* for inclusion in our next edition.

Have fun and please share your results with us.

HOW TO READ PHOTO JOLTS!

Each activity starts with an italicized header. It's a one-sentence question that drives each Photo Jolts! activity.

This paragraph explains why the above question is important or useful.

SYNOPSIS

The 'Synopsis' section summarizes what participants do during this activity.

PURPOSE

The 'Purpose' section explains what we wish to accomplish with this activity. Each activity can create clarity, inspire creativity, or provoke conversation.

> ! *Clarity*: How are we bringing clarity to a topic?
> ! *Creativity*: How are we inspiring creative processes?
> ! *Conversation*: How are we provoking deeper conversations?

Know your purpose when you start an activity. And yes, you can use a single activity to accomplish all three.

TRAINING TOPICS

The 'Training Topics' section lists appropriate courses, subjects, and environments for this activity. This list is not comprehensive. While we list our top five or six training topics for each activity, you can – and should – customize these *Photo Jolts!* to suit your training topic. To view a comprehensive topics cross-reference, refer to *Table D* (pg. 358).

- *Solo*: An individual engages in reflective learning.

- *One-on-One Coaching*: Explore, provoke, and discuss your client's thoughts, feelings, and ideas.
- *Icebreaker*: Inject energy and interaction into an event.
- *Art*: Get participants using their eyes, hands, and brains while drawing.
- *Business*: Explore important business issues.
- *Communication*: Discover the best approaches to communicating with others.
- *Creativity*: Generate new ideas, more ideas, and better ideas.
- *Culture, Diversity, Perception*: Explore new and different viewpoints.
- *Customer Service*: Explore ways to understand and enhance customer experiences.
- *Design:* Identify visual and non-visual designs that improve the look and function of your products or solutions.
- *Interviewing*: Discover ways to interview for information, for decision-making, or to find the perfect candidate.
- *Language / Vocabulary:* Test your use of vocabulary in any language.
- *Leadership (Politics and Power, Strategic Thinking)*: Identify strategies that lead others into the future.
- *Observation Skills:* Develop your ability to notice significant details in environments and situations.
- *Philosophy*: Consider the fundamental nature of reality.
- *Problem solving, Critical Thinking, Decision-making*: Find the best solutions to the problems and opportunities you face.
- *Psychology / Emotional Intelligence / Memory & Brain Training*: Explore human thought and behavior.

- *Recommended for Kids:* Help children increase clarity, creativity, and conversation while having fun.
- *Sales and Marketing*: Identify market-friendly approaches.
- *Sciences*: Think systematically like a scientist.
- *Teamwork*: Build high-functioning teams.
- *Training*: Open, close, or deepen a learning experience.

PARTICIPANTS

The 'Participants' section lists the:

- *Minimum*: This is the minimum number of participants to run a Photo Jolt. Since more than forty of these *Photo Jolts!* work in solitaire mode, this number is often 1.
- *Maximum*: This is the workable maximum number of participants for one facilitator.
- *Best*: This is the 'best' number of participants for this activity. This number is based on our experience in running these exercises to achieve the purpose of the activity.
- *Configurations*: These are the configurations that this exercise works best for. Options include 'Solo', 'Pairs', 'Triads', and 'Groups'. We define 'Groups' as 4 participants or more.

Please use these numbers as a guideline, not a rule. With minor adjustments, enough cards, and enough facilitators, you can run a Photo Jolt with any number of participants.

TIME

The 'Time' section recommends a standard range of time for this activity. Again, this is a guideline, not a rule. Most *Photo Jolts!* take less than 5 minutes using pairs. Similarly, any Photo Jolt can last 2 to 4 hours, depending on the number of participants and the depth of the debrief.

- ⏰ *< 5 minutes*: Solo/pair energizers with little debrief discussion.
- ⏰ *5 to 15 minutes*: Pair/triad sharing. Short debrief.
- ⏰ *15 to 30 minutes*: Group sharing. Full debriefs.
- ⏰ *30 to 60 minutes*: Multiple rounds, deeper debriefs, debate, and exploration.
- ⏰ *60 minutes or more*: Combine multiple rounds or sequences to cover multiple learning points.

Customize each activity to fit your needs.

- *Make Photo Jolts! longer*: by adding additional rounds, increasing the range of sharing, combining *Photo Jolts!* to create sequences, or increasing the number of debrief questions and answers.
- *Make Photo Jolts! shorter*: by removing rounds, allowing only pair sharing, dropping steps, or reducing the number of debrief questions and answers.

PREPARATION

The 'Preparation' section lists actions, supplies, and room requirements for each activity. Typical preparation steps include sorting images, clearing table space, and printing worksheets.

Supplies called for in this book include:

- *Photo Jolts!* Cards (or alternative image cards). In this book, we assume that a deck of cards = 54 images.
- Worksheets (download from *http://PhotoJolts.com*)
- Pens, Markers, or Pencils
- Paper
- Flipcharts

- Sticky Notes
- Dice

ANYWHERE JOLTS! are highlighted because they work anywhere: standing up, in a car, at a desk or table, or virtually.

VIRTUAL FACILITATION OPTIONS

The 'Virtual Facilitation Options' section recommends approaches to facilitate remote participants:

- ✓ *Image Sharing without Cards*: Run these *Photo Jolts!* by choosing sharing images with local and remote participants via video or desktop sharing. This requires display capabilities in the remote locations. Participants use the same core image(s). Alternatively, ask participants to use the image set at
  http://pinterest.com/smartashell/photojolts/
- ✓ *Video Sharing with Cards*: Run these *Photo Jolts!* by providing each virtual location with a deck of images and a video link.
- ✓ *Audio Sharing with Cards*: Run these *Photo Jolts!* by providing each virtual location with a deck of images. The virtual participants describe their images without sharing them via video.
- ✓ *Remote Facilitation with Cards*: If the minimum numbers of participants are present at the remote location, run these *Photo Jolts!* locally and then debrief globally.
- ✓ *No Virtual Facilitation*: These *Photo Jolts!* do not work well in virtual environments. Fortunately, this circumstance is rare.

FLOW

The 'Flow' section lists the steps recommended for this activity.

1. *Task 1*. Description of task 1.
2. *Task 2*. Description of task 2.
3. *Task 3*. Description of task 3.

VARIATIONS

These fifty-one *Photo Jolts!* contain more than 300 additional variations. The 'Variations' section suggests ways to customize this activity in the interest of time, complexity, or intent. Typical variations make the activity more or less difficult, more or less game-like, or more topic-specific.

- *Variation A*: Description of variation.
- *Variation B*: Description of variation.

PLAY SAMPLE

The 'Play Sample' section provides sample images and responses for the activity. The sample appears in 'bullet points' if the responses are random.

- Response A
- Response B
- Response C

The sample appears in a numbered list if the responses are ordered.

1. Response 1, then
2. Response 2, then
3. Response 3

DEBRIEF QUESTIONS

The 'Debrief Questions' section suggests approaches and questions for a debrief session. The suggestions are neither complete nor comprehensive. Use these as a starting point to create your own debrief questions or skip the debrief questions if you're using *Photo Jolts!* as an icebreaker activity.

- Debrief Question 1
- Debrief Question 2
- Debrief Question 3

RESOURCES

The 'Resources' section lists useful videos, books, and websites.

- *Resource Type*: Resource 1
- *Resource Type*: Resource 2

WORKSHEETS

The 'Worksheets' section lists worksheets that are recommended for use with the activity. Download *Photo Jolts!* worksheets from *http://PhotoJolts.com*

Photo Examples

Below are six images from the *Photo Jolts!* card deck. These examples are typical of strong *Photo Jolts!* images. They are high-resolution, high-impact, immersive, ambiguous, varied, and global in nature.

Download full-color versions of these images in the *Photo Jolts! Supplement* at *http://PhotoJolts.com*.

Photograph 1 – Skyscraper

Photograph 2 – Female Runners

Photograph 3 – Ribbons

Photograph 4 – Bloody Fish

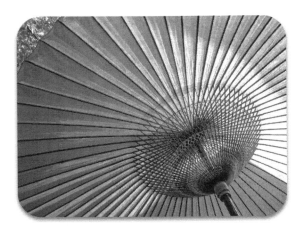

Photograph 5 – Umbrella

Photograph 6 – Nature Path

PART TWO

PHOTO JOLTS! ACTIVITIES

01

PHOTO JOLTED!

Which image 'Jolts' you?

We go through our days repeating ingrained patterns until we're jolted by something new and interesting. Which photo 'Jolts' you?

SYNOPSIS

Participants select a photograph that 'Jolts' them. They share the photo with other participants and explain why they chose it.

PURPOSE

! *Clarity*: Bring participants into the present.

! *Creativity*: Stimulate right-brain activity.

! *Conversation*: Discuss what 'Jolts' participants.

TRAINING TOPICS

- *Solo*: What 'Jolts' me?
- *One-on-One Coaching*: What 'Jolts' you?
- *Icebreaker*: What 'Jolts' those around me?
- *Communication*: How can I use images to 'Jolt' an audience?
- *Culture, Diversity, Perspective*: How – and why – do images 'Jolt' us differently?
- *Psychology*: Why does something 'Jolt' me? Does it 'Jolt' others?

PARTICIPANTS

- *Minimum*: 1
- *Maximum*: 50
- *Best*: 6 to 20
- *Configurations*: Solo, Pairs, Triads, or Groups

TIME

- *< 5 minutes*: Run in pairs or triads. Short or no debrief.
- *5 to 15 minutes*: Run in groups of 10 or less. Debrief.
- *15 to 30 minutes*: Run in a large group of 10 to 30. Debrief.

PREPARATION

- Provide one deck of *Photo Jolts!* cards per 12 participants.
- Spread out the *Photo Jolts!* images on an open table or surface.

VIRTUAL FACILITATION OPTIONS (SEE PAGE 21)

- ✓ Video Sharing with Cards
- ✓ Audio Sharing with Cards
- ✓ Remote Facilitation with Cards

FLOW

1. *Set the stage*. Ask participants to silently choose a photo that 'Jolts' them.
2. *Choose photographs*. Participants silently choose a photo. The facilitator should also choose one. Allow 1 to 2 minutes.
3. *Return to seats*. After choosing images, participants should return to their seats to indicate they are finished. The facilitator may need to start a countdown – "One minute left" – to encourage participants to return to their seats.
4. *Describe each image and metaphor*. The facilitator demonstrates the method for describing the images. First, hold up the *Photo Jolts!* card and show it to the participants without comment. Second, describe the literal image. Third, describe why this photo 'Jolts' you.
5. *Continue.* All participants share their images and explain why theirs jolted them.
6. *Debrief*. Debrief the activity.

For large groups: Large groups are best facilitated as smaller groups of 6 – 10 participants. After the groups have shared, ask them to choose the best image in their group. The fastest method we have found is to ask members of each small group to point to their favorite response on the count of three. The winning member of each group then shares his or her metaphorical image with the large group.

VARIATIONS

- *Love / Hate*: What do you love in this picture? How can you bring what you love into your situation or topic? What do you hate in this picture? How can you remove what you hate from your situation or topic?

- *Image Thief*: Move around the room and steal any image you want. You must give your image to the person you stole from. An image can only be stolen three times. Debrief the dynamics of the activity.

- *Clockwork Orange*: The facilitator displays a single image. Ask participants to identify what elements of this photo 'Jolt' them.

PLAY SAMPLE

Here is an example using *Photograph 1 - Skyscraper*.

- A participant shows the skyscraper image to others without comment.

- The participant says, "This is a skyscraper."
- The participant continues, "This photo 'Jolts' me because I was afraid of heights. I overcame that fear by learning mountain climbing skills on my weekends."

DEBRIEF OPTIONS

Often, no debrief is required. Simply use this Photo Jolt as an icebreaker or as an introduction to other activities. It can, however, act as a training tool. To further debrief this Photo Jolt, ask these questions:

- *How did each of you define 'Jolt'?*
- *What common themes (or paradoxes) did we surface?*
- *What surprised you in the responses?*

If this activity is a warm-up for training or a meeting, refer back to the findings as appropriate; "As Chris mentioned during our Photo Jolt, we should take control of our fears if we want to be successful. What are our fears with this new project?"

Poker Jolts! cards spread out on a table

02

A THOUSAND WORDS

Which image best captures your situation or topic?

It's said that a picture is worth a thousand words. Some add that a metaphor is worth a thousand pictures. Which photograph best captures your 'thousand-thousand' words for this situation or topic?

SYNOPSIS

Participants select a photograph that expresses their situation or topic. Later they share the metaphorical image with other participants.

PURPOSE

- ! *Clarity*: Convert ambiguous words into concrete images.
- ! *Creativity*: Apply metaphorical thinking to a situation or topic.
- ! *Conversation*: Share thoughts on a situation or topic.

TRAINING TOPICS

- *Solo*: How do I view this situation?
- *One-on-One Coaching*: How do you view this situation?
- *Icebreaker*: How do others view this situation or topic?
- *Creativity*: What metaphor best fits this situation or topic?
- *Any training topic (see Table A):* How do students view this topic?

PARTICIPANTS

- † *Minimum*: 1
- † *Maximum*: Any number
- † *Best*: 6 to 50
- † *Configurations*: Solo, Pairs, Triads, or Groups

TIME

- ⏲ *< 5 minutes*: Run in pairs or triads. Debrief.
- ⏲ *5 to 15 minutes*: Run in groups of 10 or less. Debrief.
- ⏲ *15 to 30 minutes*: Run in a large group (10 to 30). Encourage deep discussion.

PREPARATION

- Provide one deck of *Photo Jolts!* cards per 12 participants.
- Spread out the *Photo Jolts!* images on an open table or surface.
- *ANYWHERE JOLT!* Run this Photo Jolt standing up, in a car, at a desk or table, or virtually.

VIRTUAL FACILITATION OPTIONS (SEE PAGE 21)

- ✓ Video Sharing with Cards
- ✓ Audio Sharing with Cards
- ✓ Remote Facilitation with Cards

FLOW

1. *Define the situation or topic.* Introduce the participants to the situation or topic of your meeting, workshop, or event (see *Table A* for possible topics).

2. *Choose photographs.* Participants silently choose a photo that acts as a metaphor for the situation or topic. The facilitator also chooses a photo. Allow 1 to 2 minutes.

3. *Return to seats.* After choosing images, participants should return to their seats to indicate they are finished.

4. *Describe each image and metaphor.* The facilitator demonstrates the method for describing the images. First, hold up the *Photo Jolts!* card and show it to the participants without comment. Second, describe the literal image. Third, describe how it is a metaphor for the current situation or topic.

5. *Continue.* All participants share their images and metaphors.

6. *Debrief.* Debrief the activity

For large groups: Large groups are best facilitated as smaller groups of 6 – 10 participants. After the groups have shared, ask them to choose the best metaphorical image in their group. The fastest method we have found is to ask members of each small group to point to their favorite response on the count of three. The winning member of each group then shares his or her metaphorical image with the large group.

VARIATIONS

- *Vary the Situation/Topic*: See *Table A* for a list of potential topics.
- *Collective Choice*: Form teams of three to five participants. Teams collectively choose one card representing the topic.
- *Appreciation*: Identify a partner whose contribution you appreciate. Choose an image that represents what you appreciate about them. Share the image and metaphor. Watch an example of this exercise with authors Nancy Duarte and Garr Reynolds at *http://YouTube.com/SMARTasHellVideos*

PLAY SAMPLE

Here is an example using *Photograph 1 - Skyscraper* as a response to the challenge, "Choose a photo that is a metaphor for leadership."

- A participant shows the skyscraper image to the other participants without comment.

- The participant describes the literal image, "This is a skyscraper surrounded by clouds and fog."
- The participant completes the metaphor, "This is a metaphor for leadership because leaders must rise above the fog and clouds to see the long view. Others then use that vision as a way to gain clarity."

DEBRIEF QUESTIONS

Often, no debrief is required. Simply use this Photo Jolt as an introduction or icebreaker for other activities. To further debrief this Photo Jolt, ask these questions:

- *What common themes did we see in our images?*
- *What paradoxes did we surface during our sharing?*
- *What surprised you in the responses?*

If this Photo Jolt is used for training or a meeting, refer back to the findings as appropriate; "As Joey mentioned during our Photo Jolt, followers expect a leader to 'rise above the fog'. What does that mean to you?"

RESOURCES

- *Photo Jolts! Video*: See examples of *A Thousand Words* at *http://YouTube.com/SMARTasHellVideo*
- *Photo Jolts! Video*: Watch authors Nancy Duarte and Garr Reynolds play *Appreciation* at *http://YouTube.com/SMARTasHellVideo*

USE CASE

What is Performance Improvement?

'A Thousand Words' is the classic Photo Jolts! activity. It works for any topic, any situation, and any audience.

In 2013, I attended the International Society for Performance Improvement's annual conference in Reno, Nevada. I wanted attendees to explain what 'Performance Improvement' meant to them, so I asked members to pick a card and share with us.

Visit http://YouTube.com/SMARTasHellVideo to watch three great responses from performance specialists Emily Blunt, David Timby, and Michael Papay.

- Glenn

03

ANOTHER THOUSAND WORDS

Which images best show similarities and contrasts?

While definitions are helpful, we can gain additional insights by comparing and contrasting two sides of a situation or topic.

SYNOPSIS

Participants select two photographs that express dualities within their situation or topic. Later they describe the metaphorical images to other participants.

PURPOSE

- ! *Clarity*: Compare and contrast two key themes.
- ! *Creativity*: Expand our view of a situation or topic.
- ! *Conversation*: Provoke safe debate about best approaches.

TRAINING TOPICS

- *Solo*: What dualities do I view in this situation?
- *One-on-One Coaching*: What dualities do you view in this situation?
- *Icebreaker*: What dualities do others view in this situation or topic?
- *Creativity*: How many similarities or differences can I see in this situation or topic?
- *Philosophy*: What is a dichotomy? Are all things similar? Are all things different?
- *Any training topic (see Table B):* How do the students see this subject?

PARTICIPANTS

- † *Minimum*: 1
- † *Maximum*: 50
- † *Best*: 6 to 20
- † *Configurations*: Solo, Pairs, Triads, or Groups

TIME

- ⏰ *< 5 minutes*: Run 'lightning rounds' in pairs.
- ⏰ *5 to 15 minutes*: Run in pairs or triads. Debrief.
- ⏰ *15 to 30 minutes*: Run in groups. Debrief.

🕐 *30 to 60 minutes*: 'Walk and Share' with 10 other participants. Encourage deep discussion of the similarities and contrasts found in the situation or topic.

PREPARATION

- Provide one deck of *Photo Jolts!* cards per 8 participants.
- Spread out the *Photo Jolts!* images on an open table or surface.
- *ANYWHERE JOLT!* Run this Photo Jolt standing up, in a car, at a desk or table, or virtually.

VIRTUAL FACILITATION OPTIONS (SEE PAGE 21)

✓ Video Sharing with Cards
✓ Audio Sharing with Cards
✓ Remote Facilitation with Cards

FLOW

1. *Define the situation or topic*. Introduce the participants to the situation or topic of your meeting, workshop, or event.
2. *Choose photographs*. Participants silently choose two photos that address a comparison or contrast – *Leadership vs. Management, Speed vs. Quality, Creativity vs. Process, Independence vs. Interdependence*, etc. The facilitator also chooses two photos. Allow 1 to 2 minutes.
3. *Return to seats*. After choosing images, participants should return to their seats to indicate they are finished.
4. *Describe the first image and metaphor*. The facilitator demonstrates the method for describing the images. First, hold up the first *Photo Jolts!* card and show it to the participants without comment. Second, describe the literal image. Third, describe how it is a metaphor for the situation or topic.

5. *Describe the second image and metaphor*. Next, repeat the process for your second card.

6. *Continue*. All participants share their images and metaphors.

7. *Debrief*. Debrief the activity.

VARIATIONS

- *Vary the Situation/Topic*: See *Table B* for a list of potential topics.

- *Assembled Choice*: Form pairs. Player one chooses an image for the first topic (*Management*, for example). Player two chooses an image for the second topic (*Leadership*, for example). Share metaphors and discuss the results.

- *Collective Choice*: Form teams of three to five participants. Teams collectively choose two cards; one representing each topic.

- *Staggered Choice*: Open the session with participants choosing the 'base' image (for example, *Leading*). Debrief that subject fully. Later in the session, participants choose the contrasting metaphor (for example *Following*).

- *Dichotomies*: Deal two random images. Brainstorm as many dichotomies as possible, based on those two images.

PLAY SAMPLE

Here is an example using *Photograph 3 – Ribbons* and *Photograph 1 – Skyscraper*. The photographs were chosen as a response to the challenge, "Pick two photos: one that represents management and one that represents leadership."

- A participant shows the colored ribbons to the participants, saying, "This is an image of many pieces of ribbon. It is a metaphor for management because managers have to pay attention to the details of many different tasks and they need to discern subtle differences in similar things."
- The participant then shows the skyscraper, saying, "This is a skyscraper surrounded by clouds and fog. It is a metaphor for leadership because leaders must rise above the fog and clouds to see the long view. Others then use that vision as a way to gain clarity."

DEBRIEF QUESTIONS

To get the most out of this Photo Jolt, ask these questions:

- *What common themes did we see in our images?*
- *What paradoxes did we surface during our sharing?*
- *What surprised you in the responses?*
- *Are our responses similar to each other or different from each other?*

If this Photo Jolt is a warm-up for training or a meeting, refer back to the findings as appropriate; "As Pat mentioned during our Photo Jolt, managers pay attention to details. What details are the most difficult to track?"

04

A CHRISTMAS CAROL

What would the past, present, and future 'ghosts' of your situation tell you?

In Charles Dickens' *A Christmas Carol*, Ebenezer Scrooge learns important lessons from the ghosts of Christmas past, present, and future. What would your ghosts tell you about your situation?

SYNOPSIS

Participants select three photographs that express the past, present, and future of their situation or topic. Later they share the metaphorical images with other participants.

PURPOSE

! *Clarity*: Reflect on the status of a situation over time.

! *Creativity*: Listen to ghosts of your past, present, and future.

! *Conversation*: Share viewpoints on the history, the current state, and the desired future of an organization, relationship, project, or product.

TRAINING TOPICS

- *Solo*: How has my situation changed over time? What is my vision of the future?

- *One-on-One Coaching*: How has your situation changed over time? What is your vision of the future?

- *Leadership*: What is my vision of the future?

- *Teamwork*: How has our team situation changed over time?

- *Any training topic (see Table A)*: What is the history and future of our topic?

PARTICIPANTS

- *Minimum*: 1
- *Maximum*: 50 (use the *Collective Choice* variation)
- *Best*: 6 to 20
- *Configurations*: Solo, Pairs, Triads, or Groups

TIME

- *5 to 15 minutes*: Run in pairs or triads. No debrief.
- *15 to 30 minutes*: Run in groups. Short Debrief.
- *30 to 60 minutes*: Run in large groups. Debrief with *Gallery Tour* variation.

🕐 *60 minutes or more*: Combine with *Photo Jolt! 05 Building the Bridge* for a 2-to-4-hour workshop.

PREPARATION

- Provide one deck of *Photo Jolts!* cards per 6 participants.
- Spread out the *Photo Jolts!* images on an open table or surface.
- Ask participants to clear table space for this Photo Jolt.
- <Optional> Provide wall space where the participants can create a viewing gallery.

VIRTUAL FACILITATION OPTIONS (SEE PAGE 21)

✓ Video Sharing with Cards

✓ Audio Sharing with Cards

✓ Remote Facilitation with Cards

FLOW

1. *Define the situation or topic.* Introduce the participants to the situation or topic of your meeting, workshop, or event (see *Table A* for possible topics).

2. *Choose photographs.* Participants silently choose three photographs that address the situation or topic: one photograph represents the past state of the topic; one photograph represents the current state of the topic; and one photograph represents the desired future state of the topic. The facilitator should also choose three images. Allow 2 to 3 minutes.

3. *Return to seats.* After choosing their images, participants should return to their seats to indicate they are finished.

4. *Describe the first image and metaphor.* The facilitator demonstrates the method for describing the images. Hold up the first *Photo Jolts!* card and show it to the participants without

comment. Describe the literal image. Describe how it is a metaphor for the past situation or topic.

5. *Describe the second image and metaphor*. Next, repeat the process for the present situation, using your second card.

6. *Describe the third image and metaphor*. Next, repeat the process for the future situation, using your third card.

7. *Continue*. Participants now share their images and metaphors. Allow one minute per participant.

8. *Debrief*. Debrief the activity.

For large groups: Ask each table group to choose the 'best' metaphorical images (the fastest method is to ask members of each table group to point to the best one on the count of three) and then share them with the room.

VARIATIONS

- *Assembled Choice*: Form triads. One team member picks the past, one picks the present, and one picks the future. Share metaphors and discuss the results.

- *Collective Choice*: Form teams of three to five participants. Collectively choose three cards representing the past, present, and future.

- *Staggered Choice*: Open the session with participants choosing and sharing a metaphor for the past situation. Next, have them choose and share their metaphor for the current situation. Finally, ask the participants to choose and share their metaphor for the future metaphor/vision.

- *Gallery Tour*: Participants build their past, present, and future stories and hang them on the wall. Conduct a gallery tour, while each creator explains his or her story. This is a great way to get participants out of their chairs.

PLAY SAMPLE

Here is an example using *Photograph 3 – Ribbons, Photograph 4 – Bloody Fish*, and *Photograph 1 – Skyscraper*. The photographs were chosen as a response to the challenge, "Choose three photos: one that represents our past leadership style, one that represents our current leadership style, and one that represents our desired leadership style."

- *Past*: A participant shows the colored ribbons to the other participants, "This is an image of many pieces of ribbon. It is a metaphor for our past leadership style because we paid attention to the details of many different tasks and directed you on how to do them."

- *Present*: The participant shows the bloody fish and continues, "This is an image of fish that are cut up and bleeding. It is a metaphor for our current leadership situation. We've tried to create a better company by being more 'hands-off'. As a result, people are making mistakes and spilling a little blood. We're okay with that. Mistakes are a part of learning."

- *Future*: The participant shows the skyscraper and finishes, "This is a skyscraper surrounded by clouds and fog. It is a metaphor for my desired leadership style. We, as leaders must rise above the fog and clouds to see the long view. Others can then use our vision as a way to gain clarity. The pain we feel today will lead to greatness tomorrow."

DEBRIEF QUESTIONS

To get the most out of this Photo Jolt, ask these questions:

- *What common themes did we identify in our images?*
- *What differences or conflicts did we surface in our images?*
- *How can we explain these differences?*
- *Some of you weren't here in the past. What are your thoughts as you listen?*
- *What surprised you in the responses?*
- *Which time period was most difficult: past, present, or future? Why?*

RESOURCES

- *Reading*: Read *A Christmas Carol* at *Literature.org*
- *Photo Jolts! Video*: Watch Glenn and Thiagi demonstrate *A Christmas Carol* and see more *Photo Jolts!* videos at *http://YouTube.com/SMARTasHellVideo*

USE CASE
Virtual Facilitation

When I was asked to demonstrate Photo Jolts! on Robert Thompson's radio show 'Thought Grenades', it presented a great opportunity to show how an activity is conducted virtually.

With Robert in Northern California and his co-host Mike Neiss in Michigan, I facilitated the future portion of 'A Christmas Carol', using Photo Jolts! images on Pinterest. Listen as they explain what they want to achieve with 'Thought Grenades' at http://tinyurl.com/mm4l964

- Glenn

05

BUILDING THE BRIDGE

How do we build a bridge from our current situation to our desired future?

It's easy – and tempting – to spend hours, days, even years talking about how bad things are today or how great we wish they could be in the future. How do we identify the actions that move us from 'here' to 'there'?

SYNOPSIS

Participants select two photographs that express the current status and desired future of their situation or topic. They then select photographs representing the actions that will close the gap.

PURPOSE

- ! *Clarity*: Align on the current status, the desired future, and possible action steps.
- ! *Creativity*: Brainstorm actions for change.
- ! *Conversation*: Discuss the desired future of an organization, relationship, project, or product.

TRAINING TOPICS

- *Solo*: How can I build a bridge from where I am to where I want to be?
- *One-on-One Coaching*: How can you build a bridge from where you are to where you want to be?
- *Leadership*: How can we reach our desired future state?
- *Problem Solving*: What is the best way for us to reach our desired future state?
- *Teamwork*: How can we work together to realize our vision?

PARTICIPANTS

- † *Minimum*: 1
- † *Maximum*: 50 (use the *Collective Choice* variation)
- † *Best*: 6 to 20
- † *Configurations*: Solo, Pairs, Triads, or Groups

TIME

- *5 to 15 minutes*: Run in pairs or triads. Short debrief.
- *15 to 30 minutes*: Run in groups of 10 or less. Full debrief.
- *30 to 60 minutes*: Run *Gallery Tour* variation.
- *60 minutes or more*: Combine with *Photo Jolt! 04 A Christmas Carol* to create a 2-to-4-hour workshop.

PREPARATION

- Provide one deck of *Photo Jolts!* cards per 5 participants.
- Spread out the *Photo Jolts!* images on an open table or surface.
- Ask participants to clear table space for this Photo Jolt.
- <Optional> Provide sticky notes for commenting.
- <Optional> Create wall space where the participants can hang their images to create a gallery for viewing.

VIRTUAL FACILITATION OPTIONS (SEE PAGE 21)

- ✓ Video Sharing with Cards
- ✓ Audio Sharing with Cards
- ✓ Remote Facilitation with Cards

FLOW

1. *Define the situation or topic.* Introduce the participants to the situation or topic of your meeting, workshop, or event (see *Table A* for possible topics).

2. *Choose 'current' & 'future' photographs.* Participants silently choose two photographs that address the situation or topic: one photograph represents the current state of the topic, and one photograph represents the desired future state of the topic. The facilitator should also choose two images. Allow 1 to 2 minutes.

3. *Return to seats.* After choosing images, participants should return to their seats to indicate they are finished.

4. *Describe the first image and metaphor.* The facilitator demonstrates the method for describing the images. First, hold up the first *Photo Jolts!* card and show it to the participants without

comment. Second, describe the literal image. Third, describe how it is a metaphor for the current situation or topic.

5. *Describe the second image and metaphor*. Repeat the process for the future situation, using your second card.

6. *Continue*. Each participant shares his or her images and metaphors.

7. *Choose 'action' photographs*. Participants silently choose one to three photographs that suggest actions for moving from the current state to the desired future state. The facilitator should also choose three. Allow 2 to 4 minutes.

8. *Return to seats*. After choosing their images, participants should return to their seats to indicate they are finished.

9. *Describe the action images and metaphors*. The facilitator demonstrates the method for describing the images.

10. *Continue*. Each participant shares his or her action images and metaphors.

11. *Debrief*. Debrief the activity.

For large groups: Ask each table group to choose the best metaphorical images (the fastest method is to ask members of each table group to point to the 'best' on the count of three) and then share them with the room.

VARIATIONS

- *Collective Choice*: Form teams of three to five participants. Ask each team to collectively choose their cards.

- *Staggered Choice*: Open the session with participants choosing and sharing the present state. In the middle of the session, have them choose the future metaphor. Close the session by choosing the actions that will 'build the bridge'.

- *Gallery Tour*: Ask participants to create their 'bridge' story and hang it on the wall. When finished, participants conduct a gallery tour, while the creator explains the story. This is a great way to get participants out of their chairs.

- ***Combine with A Christmas Carol***: Participants tell their 'Past, Present, Future' story before identifying the necessary actions to reach the desired future state by completing *Photo Jolt! 04 – A Christmas Carol.*

PLAY SAMPLE

Here is an example using *Photograph 4 – Bloody Fish, Photograph 2 – Female Runners*, and *Photograph 1 – Skyscraper*. These photographs were chosen as a response to the challenge, "Choose two photos: one that represents our current environment and one that represents our desired environment. Then choose an image that suggests actions that help us reach our desired state."

- A participant shows the bloody fish image. "This is an image of fish that are cut up and bleeding. It is a metaphor for our current environment. Dead fish are washing up on our beaches every day."

- The participant shows the women running in a rainstorm. "I want to have a clean environment, with no fear of toxins from automobiles or acid rain."

- The participant shows the skyscraper image. "To achieve our goal, we'll need to make corporations our partners, not our enemies."

DEBRIEF QUESTIONS

To get the most out of this Photo Jolt, ask these questions:

- *What common themes did we see in our images?*
- *What paradoxes did we surface during our sharing?*
- *What surprised you in the responses?*
- *Which actions are worth pursuing?*

Photo Jolts! co-author Thiagi shares his metaphor for learning
http://YouTube.com/SMARTasHellVideo

06
PERSPECTIVES

Do we <u>see</u> the same thing when we <u>look</u> at the same thing?

It's said that a picture is worth a thousand words. Those thousand words are enough to create alignment if we see the same thing in an image. But do we really see the same thing?

SYNOPSIS

Participants select photographs that express their situation or topic. They then silently interpret the images and share what they found.

PURPOSE

> ! *Clarity*: Expose differences in interpretation.
>
> ! *Creativity*: Explore how perspective breeds variety.
>
> ! *Conversation*: Discuss the effect of perspective and interpretation.

TRAINING TOPICS

- *Icebreaker*: How do we interpret images differently?

- *Communication*: Are we really communicating what we think we're communicating?

- *Culture, Diversity, Perspective*: How does culture effect perspective? How do different perspectives or interpretations bring value?

- *Customer Service*: How do our perceptions of good or bad service differ?

- *Teamwork*: How do your teammates interpret images differently from you?

PARTICIPANTS

- *Minimum*: 2
- *Maximum*: Any number
- *Best*: 10 to 20
- *Configurations*: Pairs, Triads, or Groups

TIME

- *5 to 15 minutes*: Run in pairs or triads. Short debrief.
- *15 to 30 minutes*: Run in small teams. Full debrief.
- *30 to 60 minutes*: Run two rounds. Small or large teams. Full debrief.

PREPARATION

- Provide one deck of *Photo Jolts!* cards per 12 participants.
- Provide one *Perspectives Worksheet* per participant
- Spread out the *Photo Jolts!* images on an open table or surface.

VIRTUAL FACILITATION OPTIONS (SEE PAGE 21)

✓ Video Sharing without Cards
✓ Remote Facilitation with Cards

FLOW

1. *Define the situation or topic.* Introduce the participants to the situation or topic of your meeting, workshop, or event (see *Table A* for possible topics).

2. *Choose photographs.* Participants silently choose a photograph that acts as a metaphor for the situation or topic. The facilitator should also choose one. Allow 1 to 2 minutes.

3. *Return to seats.* After choosing images, participants should return to their seats to indicate they are finished.

4. *Describe the image and metaphor.* The facilitator demonstrates the method for describing the images. First, hold up the *Photo Jolts!* card and show it to participants without comment. Second, describe the literal image. Third, describe how it is a metaphor for the current situation or topic.

5. *Start Perspectives Worksheet.* Participants now complete the top row of the *Perspectives Worksheet*, by writing their name, the literal interpretation of their image, and the metaphorical interpretation of their image. Allow 1 minute.

6. *Complete Perspectives Worksheet.* Participants silently pass their images to the participant on their right. Fill out the second row of

the *Perspectives Worksheet* for this next image. Allow 1 minute. Continue until participants have seen every image at the table.

7. *Share perspectives on first image*. Choose which participant goes first. The first participant shows their image, describes the literal image, and then describes their metaphor. Go around the table and have the other participants share their perspectives on that image. Note similarities and differences.

8. *Continue*. All participants share their images and hear alternative perspectives.

9. *Debrief*. Debrief the activity.

VARIATIONS

- *Vary the Questions*: See *Table A* for a list of potential topics for this Photo Jolt.

- *One View*: Show one image. Participants write their metaphors and then share with the group. Debrief as above.

- *Eye of the Beholder*: Deal a random card. Tell the participants that this image represents the customer service they just received. Ask them to write down their perception of the service. Share and note differences.

- *One More Metaphor*: Hold up an image and share a metaphor. Ask other participants to call out alternative metaphors. Continue brainstorming metaphors on the image until there are no more. Debrief as above.

PLAY SAMPLE

Here are various interpretations of *Photograph 1 – Skyscraper*. This photograph was chosen as a response to the challenge, "Pick a photo that is a metaphor for our current project."

1. Tracy writes, "This is a skyscraper. It shows that our project is unstable."
2. Sam writes, "This is a tower. It shows our towering achievement."
3. Pat writes, "This is a building. It shows that the weather around our project looks ominous."
4. Lou writes, "This is a tower. It demonstrates that we've got a huge project ahead of us."

What other interpretations can you imagine?

DEBRIEF QUESTIONS

To get the most out of this Photo Jolt, ask these questions:

- *How similar or different were our literal interpretations?*
- *How similar or different were our metaphorical interpretations?*
- *Why were they different or similar?*
- *What images created the biggest differences? Why?*
- *What surprised you in the responses?*
- *What are the risks in these different perspectives?*
- *How can we limit these risks?*
- *What are the advantages of these different perspectives?*
- *How can we leverage these advantages?*
- *How does this occur in our work? Slides? Communications? Interpretations of events? Interpretations of behavior?*
- *What should we do differently, based on what we learned today?*

If this Photo Jolt is a warm-up for training or a meeting, refer back to the findings where appropriate; "As Jun mentioned during our Photo Jolt, our project is unstable. How can we fix that issue?"

RESOURCES

- ☞ **Perspectives Worksheet**: Download *Photo Jolts!* worksheets from *http://PhotoJolts.com*

PERSPECTIVES WORKSHEET

Name:

Image 1

    Literal Interpretation

    Metaphorical Interpretation

Image 2

    Literal Interpretation

    Metaphorical Interpretation

Image 3

    Literal Interpretation

    Metaphorical Interpretation

Image 4

    Literal Interpretation

    Metaphorical Interpretation

Image 5

    Literal Interpretation

    Metaphorical Interpretation

07

EMOTIONAL RESCUE

Can you accurately communicate emotion through images?

We expect others will react to stimuli the same way that we do. Is that true?

SYNOPSIS

Participants choose an image to express an emotion. Other participants then guess the emotion being communicated.

PURPOSE

! *Clarity*: Convert ambiguous emotions into concrete images.

! *Creativity*: Convey emotions through metaphorical images.

! *Conversation*: Discuss the varied perspectives we bring to images and emotions.

TRAINING TOPICS

- *One-on-One Coaching*: How well can you read or communicate emotions visually?

- *Communication*: Can we communicate emotions with visuals? What emotions are my visuals communicating?

- *Culture, Diversity, Perspective*: Does culture effect meaning? If so, how?

- *Interviewing*: Does a candidate display emotional intelligence?

- *Psychology (Emotional Intelligence)*: How strong is my emotional vocabulary?

PARTICIPANTS

- *Minimum*: 1
- *Maximum*: any number (in pairs or triads)
- *Best*: 6 to 24
- *Configurations*: Pairs or Triads

TIME

- *< 5 minutes*: Run in pairs. No debrief.
- *5 to 15 minutes*: Run two rounds in pairs. Debrief.
- *15 to 30 minutes*: Run full version in triads. Debrief.
- *30 to 60 minutes*: Combine with mini-lecture or start with *Name that Emotion* variation.

PREPARATION

- Provide one deck of *Photo Jolts!* cards per team of three participants.
- Provide one *Emotional Vocabulary Worksheet* for each participant.
- *ANYWHERE JOLT!* Run this Photo Jolt standing up, in a car, at a desk or table, or virtually.

VIRTUAL FACILITATION OPTIONS (SEE PAGE 21)

✓ Remote Facilitation with Cards

FLOW

1. *Create teams*. Form teams of three.
2. *Identify emotion*. Player one thinks of an emotion and writes it on a piece of paper (optionally, provide the list of emotions in *Table C* and ask player one to choose an emotion). Player one hands this emotion to player two. Allow 1 minute.
3. *Choose photograph*. Player two reads the emotion and then chooses a photo that expresses the emotion. Player two hands this card to player three. Allow 1 to 2 minutes.
4. *Identify emotion*. Player three guesses the emotion. Player one replies with 'correct' or 'no'. Player three gets three guesses. Players two and three receive three points if they are correct on the first try, two points for the second try, one point for the third try. Allow 2 to 3 minutes.
5. *<Optional> Provide a clue*: Player two can reply "more" or "less" to a response that is close, but not exact. For example, if the emotion is "delighted," and player three says, "happy," player one can respond, "more."

6. *Rotate players*. Player two thinks of an emotion; player three chooses the photo; player one guesses. Then player three thinks of an emotion; player one chooses the photo; and player two guesses.

7. *Repeat for two more rounds*. The teams play three rounds of three emotions. The player with the most points at the end of round three wins.

8. *Debrief*. Debrief the activity.

VARIATIONS

- *Name that Emotion*: Pick a card. Name what emotion it triggers. Play this in pairs, triads, or teams as a warm-up to *Emotional Rescue*.

- *Slap that Emotion*: Lay out 10 photos. One player silently identifies a photo and chooses an emotion that it conveys. Call out the emotion. The remaining participants slap their hand down on the card that they think best matches the emotions. Participants who choose the correct image get a point.

- *Twins*: Have each participant silently choose an emotion and then identify a photo that represents the emotion. Each participant then silently pairs with someone whose emotion they think matches theirs. Share. Were they correct?

- *Team Sort*: Ask a team to silently sort all 54 photos by emotion. How many categories did they create? How did they reach agreement?

- *Reinforce*: Use this activity to reinforce team strategies and behaviors like Tuckman's Team Development Model, DISC Behavioral Assessment, or your favorite team building tool.

PLAY SAMPLE

Here is a play sample for *Photograph 4 – Bloody Fish*.

- *Player one*: Chooses the emotion 'sad'.
- *Player two*: Chooses the image of dead fish.
- *Player three*: Guesses, "Gross?"
- *Player one*: "That's not an emotion."
- *Player three*: Guesses, "Disgust?"
- *Player two*: "No. What else do you feel when you see this?"
- *Player three*: "Sad."
- *Player one*: "Correct!"
- Players two and three receive one point each.

What other emotions do you think are conveyed?

DEBRIEF QUESTIONS

To get the most out of this Photo Jolt, ask these questions:

- *How easy or hard is it for you to find an image that matches an emotion?*
- *How easy or hard is it for you to guess what emotion an image is communicating?*
- *What are your emotional blind spots?*
- *Is your emotional vocabulary shallow or deep? Why?*
- *Are there advantages to a deeper emotional vocabulary?*
- *What does this imply for visual communications?*

RESOURCES

- *Photo Jolts! Video*: Watch Glenn and Thiagi demonstrate *Emotional Rescue* and see more *Photo Jolts!* videos at *http://www.YouTube.com/SMARTasHellVideo*.
- *Emotional Rescue Table*: Download *Photo Jolts!* worksheets from *http://PhotoJolts.com*

08

USER EXPERIENCE

*How would different people experience your
product, service, or situation?*

We tend to focus on situations through the prism of
our own experience. How would others experience
our situation?

SYNOPSIS

Participants select three random *People Jolts!* cards
and explore how the people in these pictures would
experience their product, service, or situation.

PURPOSE

- ! *Clarity*: Walk in other people's shoes.
- ! *Creativity*: Generate ideas from alternative viewpoints.
- ! *Conversation*: Discuss alternative approaches to a situation.

TRAINING TOPICS

- *Solo*: How can this person help me?
- *One-on-One Coaching*: What would this person say about your situation?
- *Communication*: How would I present, speak, or write to this person?
- *Creativity*: What ideas would this person give me?
- *Culture, Diversity, Perspective*: What is this person's culture?
- *Design*: How would I design for this person?
- *Sales and Marketing*: How would I sell to this person?

PARTICIPANTS

- *Minimum*: 1
- *Maximum*: 40
- *Best*: 4 to 12
- *Configurations*: Solo, Pairs, Triads, or Groups

TIME

- *< 5 minutes*: Run one round with a mini-debrief.
- *5 to 15 minutes*: Run two rounds. Debrief.
- *15 to 30 minutes*: Run three rounds. Debrief.
- *30 to 60 minutes*: Conduct a thorough user analysis.

PREPARATION

- Provide one deck of *People Jolts!* cards for up to 50 participants.

- Alternatively, use the 14 people photos from the *Photo Jolts!* activity deck.

- *ANYWHERE JOLT!* Run this Photo Jolt standing up, in a car, at a desk or table, or virtually.

VIRTUAL FACILITATION OPTIONS (SEE PAGE 21)

- ✓ Image Sharing without Cards
- ✓ Video Sharing with Cards
- ✓ Audio Sharing with Cards
- ✓ Remote Facilitation with Cards

FLOW

1. *Define the situation or topic.* Introduce the participants to the situation or topic of your meeting, workshop, or event (see *Table A* for possible topics).

2. *Select a photograph.* Select a random photo from the *People Jolts!* deck.

3. *Shift viewpoint.* View your product, service, situation, or topic through the eyes of this user. Consider age, sex, culture, wealth, and other demographic, psychographic, and ethnographic traits. Typical questions include: What are the attributes of this person? How are you similar to this person? How are you different from this person? How would this person view your situation? What solutions or approaches would this person suggest? How can you make this person successful? Would your solutions or approaches work for this person? How would this person use your product or service? Allow 5 to 10 minutes.

4. *Choose another user.* Select another random photo and repeat Step 3.

5. *Continue.* End after assessing five different users (or when your time limit expires).

6. *Debrief.* Debrief the activity.

VARIATIONS

- *Targeted Audience*: Instead of choosing random user cards, select the audiences you are targeting. You'll gain focus, although you'll lose some creative stimulus.

"Make Work Great" author Ed Muzio shares a metaphor for his work
http://YouTube.com/SMARTasHellVideo

PLAY SAMPLE

Here are five questions or observations about a new product using
Photograph 2 - Female Runners:

- Would they prefer a product that was fashionable?
- These women might want a waterproof product.
- Is our product 'green' or natural enough for them?
- Could we get our product seen during sports broadcasts?
- Is our product sturdy enough for physical activity?

What other ideas or questions do you have?

DEBRIEF QUESTIONS

To get the most out of this Photo Jolt, ask these questions:

- *What is the value of other people's viewpoints?*
- *What insights surprised you? Why?*
- *Where they all useful? Why or why not?*
- *Whose viewpoints would be useful to your situation?*
- *Whose viewpoints would be worthless to your situation?*
- *What would happen if you listened to the useless viewpoints?*
- *Could you make the useless viewpoints useful?*
- *What actions will you take out of this exercise?*

RESOURCES

- *Photo Jolts! Video*: Watch Glenn and Thiagi demonstrate *User Experience* and see more *Photo Jolts!* videos at *http://YouTube.com/SMARTasHellVideo*

09
EMPATHY

What are people feeling?

Empathy – the ability to feel what others are feeling –
is useful to anyone who deals with people. If you're
in customer service, marketing, training, or
management, empathy is a key to success. Can you
understand what others are feeling?

SYNOPSIS

Participants select images and identify what the
people in the images are feeling or thinking.

PURPOSE

- ! *Clarity*: Understand what others are thinking or feeling.
- ! *Creativity*: Imagine what thoughts or feelings another person is experiencing.
- ! *Conversation*: Discuss the power of empathy and the difficulty of understanding someone else's experience.

TRAINING TOPICS

- *Solo*: Can I imagine what others are thinking?
- *One-on-One Coaching*: Can you imagine what others are thinking?
- *Customer Service*: Can you anticipate your customer's feelings?
- *Psychology (Emotional Intelligence)*: How well can I feel what others are feeling?
- *Sales and Marketing*: Can you speak to what others are thinking?
- *Training, Learning, Coaching*: Can you read – in real time – what others are thinking or feeling?

PARTICIPANTS

- † *Minimum*: 1
- † *Maximum*: any number
- † *Best*: 4 to 32
- † *Configurations*: Solo, Pairs, Triads, or Groups

TIME

- ⏱ *< 5 minutes*: Run in pairs. No debrief.
- ⏱ *5 to 15 minutes*: Run in triads. Debrief.
- ⏱ *15 to 30 minutes*: Conduct a deep team discussion. Debrief.

PREPARATION

- Provide one deck of *Photo Jolts!* cards per 13 participants.
- Remove all images that do not include humans.
- <Optional> Include the 8 animal images in the *Photo Jolts!* deck.
- <Optional> Use *People Jolts!* or *Animal Jolts!* decks (*http://PhotoJolts.com*)
- <Optional> Provide one copy of *Table C* to each participant.
- <Optional> Provide one *Emotional Vocabulary Worksheet* per participant.
- *ANYWHERE JOLT!* Run this Photo Jolt standing up, in a car, at a desk or table, or virtually.

VIRTUAL FACILITATION OPTIONS (see page 21)

✓ Image Sharing without Cards
✓ Remote Facilitation with Cards

FLOW

1. *Distribute photographs.* Deal a random image (depicting humans or animals) to each participant.
2. *Identify thoughts.* Identify what the person in this image is *thinking*. Allow 2 minutes.
3. *Identify feelings.* Identify what the person in this image is *feeling*. Allow 2 minutes.
4. *Identify strategies.* Create a strategy to approach this person. Allow 2 minutes.
5. *Share.* Share your thoughts and strategies with the other participants. Allow 1 minute per participant.
6. *Debrief.* Debrief the activity.

VARIATIONS

- *Anthropomorphize*: Choose an animal image. Can you imagine what an animal is thinking? Is this easier or more difficult than imagining what a human is thinking?

- *Animals and Humans*: It's often said that humans resemble their pets and vice-versa. Select an image of a human and then find an animal that matches. Explain why you see a match.

- *Mimic*: Choose an animal or person image. Hand it to your partner. Try to mimic the expression on the animal or person's face. Mimic their body language. How long can you hold that look? How does it feel?

PLAY SAMPLE

Here are five statements for *Photograph 2 – Female Runners*.

- The runners are *tired* from running so far.

- The runners are *determined* to continue in the rain.

- The runners are *worried* about possible lighting strikes.

- The runners are *thankful* for the cooling rain.

- The runners are feeling *competitive* because of the closeness of their race.

What other statements could you make?

In your opinion, which statements are most likely to be true?

DEBRIEF QUESTIONS

To get the most out of this Photo Jolt, ask these questions:

- *How easy or difficult is it to empathize with others?*
- *What is the difference between empathy and sympathy?*
- *Can you become more empathetic? If so, how?*

RESOURCES

- ☛ *Empathy Worksheet*: Download *Photo Jolts!* worksheets from *http://PhotoJolts.com*
- ☛ *Emotional Rescue Table*: Download *Photo Jolts!* worksheets from *http://PhotoJolts.com*

EMPATHY WORKSHEET

1. Image Details (Describe your image):

2. What is the subject of your image thinking?

3. What is the subject of your image feeling?

4. What are your strategies for working with this person?

    A.

    B.

    C.

10
SILENT SELECTION

How do decisions happen when there is no discussion?

Many team decisions occur with no deep discussion. Is that good or bad? How do we make decisions when we are unable to have a conversation?

SYNOPSIS

Each member of a team selects an image that is metaphorical of the topic. Silently, the group chooses the most representative image. The group then discusses the decision dynamics.

PURPOSE

! *Clarity*: See how teams work when communication is limited.

! *Creativity*: Solve a problem despite constraints.

! *Conversation*: Discuss the effects of making decisions without conversation.

TRAINING TOPICS

- *Icebreaker*: How can we work together to build our future?
- *Communication*: How much can we accomplish without talking?
- *Leadership*: How do leaders emerge?
- *Problem Solving, Decision-making, Critical Thinking*: How do we make decisions when we can't talk?
- *Psychology*: What behaviors emerge during a team challenge?
- *Teamwork*: How do things really happen on this team?

PARTICIPANTS

- *Minimum*: 4
- *Maximum*: 32
- *Best*: 8 to 24
- *Configurations*: Groups

TIME

- *5 to 15 minutes*: One round. Short debrief.
- *15 to 30 minutes*: Multiple rounds. Deep debrief.

PREPARATION

- Provide one deck of *Photo Jolts!* cards per 12 participants.
- Ask participants to clear table space for this Photo Jolt.

VIRTUAL FACILITATION OPTIONS (SEE PAGE 21)

✓ Remote Facilitation with Cards

FLOW

1. *Create teams*. Silently form teams of four to six members each.

2. *Define the situation or topic*. Introduce the participants to the situation or topic (see *Table A* for possible topics).

3. *Display topic*. Write the situation or topic on a flip chart or display it on a slide. This allows participants to read it or point at it without breaking the silence.

4. *Choose photographs*. Participants silently choose a photograph that acts as a metaphor for the situation or topic. Allow 1 to 2 minutes.

5. *Return to seats*. After choosing images, participants should return to their seats to indicate they are finished.

6. *Choose the most representative photo*. The teams silently (non-verbally, no writing allowed) reach a consensus on the most representative photo. Allow 3 minutes.

7. *Select a delegate*. Teams must silently choose a delegate.

8. *Gather the delegates*. Bring the delegates to the front of the room.

9. *Silence ends*. The delegates will now speak.

10. *Share metaphors*. Each delegate presents the team image and describes the metaphor. All 1 minute per participant.

11. *Share team strategies*. Delegates explain how their teams selected the images. Teams comment on the delegate's interpretation. Allow 3 minutes per team.

12. *Debrief*. Debrief the activity.

13. *<Optional> Round two*. Teams can apply lessons learned by running a second round. Are team dynamics improved? How?

VARIATIONS

- *Declaration*: Write down your 'most representative image' selection before the team activity starts. Turn this paper over and run the activity. Afterwards, view how the team decision differed from your choice. Are you happy with the team choice? Discuss.

PLAY SAMPLE

Here are some typical patterns seen during play:

- *Pattern A*: One or two players take over and pick a photo while others sit passively.
- *Pattern B*: No leader emerges. Little action occurs.
- *Pattern C*: Players clash because their image isn't chosen.
- *Pattern D*: Players collaborate. Participants point at the topic and point to photos. Eye contact and body language is visible among the team members.
- *Pattern E*: Teams bend the rules. They whisper or attempt to write.

DEBRIEF QUESTIONS

To get the most out of this Photo Jolt, ask these questions:

- *How did your team select their images?*
- *What worked or didn't work in this process?*
- *Was there conflict? How was it settled?*
- *Do you feel like your input was considered?*
- *How was this simulation similar to or different from what happens in your work environment?*
- *Do you feel like the best image was chosen?*
- *What would you do differently?*

11
TEAMS

How do we form teams?

Teams form (and disband) every day. What criteria do we use to build a team?

SYNOPSIS

Participants choose photos that resonate with them. They are then asked to form teams based on those images. Finally, they discuss the basis for their team formation.

PURPOSE

- ! *Clarity*: Define what makes a team.
- ! *Creativity*: Consider alternative definitions of a team.
- ! *Conversation*: Discuss and debate what creates a team.

TRAINING TOPICS

- *Icebreaker*: How do people form teams?
- *Culture, Diversity, Perspective*: How do different people define a team?
- *Problem Solving, Decision-making, Critical Thinking*: What approaches do we use to solve a problem?
- *Psychology*: What do we look for when forming a team?
- *Teamwork*: What are the characteristics of a team? How do we build an effective remote/virtual team?

PARTICIPANTS

- *Minimum*: 12
- *Maximum*: 72
- *Best*: 12 to 48
- *Configurations*: Solo, Pairs, Triads, or Groups

TIME

- *5 to 15 minutes*: Run the *Play the Hand You're Dealt* Variation. Short debrief.
- *15 to 30 minutes*: Run full version. Deep debrief on team formation.

PREPARATION

- Provide one deck of *Photo Jolts!* cards per 53 participants.
- This Photo Jolt requires that participants are able to move freely and create new teams.

VIRTUAL FACILITATION OPTIONS (SEE PAGE 21)

✓ Video Sharing with Cards

✓ Audio Sharing with Cards

✓ Remote Facilitation with Cards

FLOW

1. *Choose photographs.* Participants silently choose a photo that resonates with them. Allow 1 to 2 minutes.
2. *Return to seats.* After choosing images, participants should return to their seats to indicate they are finished.
3. *Pair and share.* Participants find a partner. Partners share why this photograph resonated with them. Allow 2 minutes.
4. *Form teams.* Participants now move around the room and use their photographs to form teams. Teams must have four and only four members. Allow 2 to 3 minutes.
5. *Share strategies.* Participants share the criteria or strategies they used to form their team.
6. *Debrief.* Debrief the activity.

VARIATIONS

- *Play the Hand You're Dealt*: Deal cards to the participants at random. Participants then move around the room and use their photographs to form teams that have four and only four members.

- *Do-over*: Participants continue *Teams* by creating new teams, based on what they've learned in the first round. Allow 5 minutes. Each team defends why their team has the best design.

- *Survival of the Fittest*: Select a judge and then propose that only one team is strong enough to live. Allow five minutes for participants to build new teams, knowing that they must fight the other teams in a 'Battle Royale'. Go! Have each team defend why their team has the best design. The judge decides the winners.

PLAY SAMPLE

Here are possible statements about the team formations:

- This team formed because we are animals.
- This team formed because the images contain water.
- This team formed because no one wanted us.
- This team formed because the images are green.

What other statements might you expect?

DEBRIEF QUESTIONS

To get the most out of this Photo Jolt, ask these questions:

- *How was your team formed?*
- *Was your team formed on the basis of similarity or differences?*
- *What are the strengths and weaknesses of a team formed with your makeup? Could a sea lion work with a lion, for example?*
- *Does your team have a mix of necessary resources - food, shelter, and tools?*
- *If you could strategize, what would you do differently?*
- *How are your teams formed in the real world?*

12

BLACK SHEEP

Which photo is <u>not</u> a member of the family?

We classify items by determining like and unlike relationships. How do we identify those relationships?

SYNOPSIS

Participants are given three photo cards. They then identify why one card is different from the other two.

PURPOSE

! *Clarity*: Explain how images are similar to or different from each other.

! *Creativity*: Create relationships among random images.

! *Conversation*: Discuss the importance of relationships and classifications to critical thinking. Discuss the ambiguity of relationships.

TRAINING TOPICS

- *Solo*: How do I group objects?
- *One-on-One Coaching*: How do you group objects?
- *Icebreaker*: How do we see groupings differently?
- *Creativity*: How can we define categories in ways that are useful?
- *Culture, Diversity, Perspective*: Is a black sheep really a black sheep?
- *Interviewing*: What strategies does a candidate use?
- *Customer Service*: What differentiates good and bad customer service?
- *Problem Solving, Decision-making, Critical Thinking*: What strategies do I use to group objects?

PARTICIPANTS

- *Minimum*: 1
- *Maximum*: any number
- *Best*: 2 to 32
- *Configurations*: Solo, Pairs, Triads, or Groups

TIME

- 🕐 *< 5 minutes*: Run in pairs. Short debrief
- 🕐 *5 to 15 minutes*: Run in triads or groups. Play multiple rounds. Full debrief.

PREPARATION

- Provide one deck of *Photo Jolts!* cards per 12 participants.
- *ANYWHERE JOLTS!* Run this Photo Jolt standing up, in a car, at a desk or table, or virtually.

VIRTUAL FACILITATION OPTIONS (SEE PAGE 21)

- ✓ Image Sharing without Cards
- ✓ Video Sharing with Cards
- ✓ Audio Sharing with Cards
- ✓ Remote Facilitation with Cards

FLOW

1. *Form triads*. Create teams of three.
2. *Deal cards*. Deal three random images to the participants.
3. *Establish relationships*. Participants silently identify two images that have a relationship, and isolate one card - the *Black Sheep* – that is different. Allow 15 to 30 seconds.
4. *Share relationships*. Participants share the relationships they identified.
5. *<Optional> Force new relationships.* Point at a card that was not chosen as the black sheep and announce, "This is the black sheep." Participants must explain why this image is the black sheep.
6. *Repeat*. Repeat the exercise two more times with new images.
7. *Debrief*. Debrief the activity.

VARIATIONS

- *Identification*: Form teams of four. Each team selects an observer. Provide the observer with private directions to note how many times each participant chooses themselves as the black sheep. Give the images to each participant personally. Play *Black Sheep*. Debrief the impact of being identified as a black sheep.

- *This Could Be You*: Use this exercise to demonstrate that Black Sheep is an arbitrary label. Lay down three cards. Point at one card and ask, "Why is *this* the black sheep?" Listen to responses. Point at the next card and ask, "Why is *this* the black sheep?" Listen to responses. Point at the third card and ask, "Why is *this* the black sheep?" Listen to responses. Debrief.

- *Good Service or Bad?* Lay down three images. Two of these images represent good customer service. One image represents bad customer service. Which one is bad? Why?

- *Combine – Lotus Blossom*: Use this exercise as a lead-in to *Photo Jolt 14 – Lotus Blossom*.

PLAY SAMPLE

Here is an example using *Photograph 1 – Skyscraper, Photograph 2 – Female Runners*, and *Photograph 3 - Ribbons*:

- *Player 1*: "The skyscraper is the black sheep because there is no color in the image."

- *Player 2*: "The running females image is the black sheep because it contains humans, while the other two do not."
- *Player 3*: "The ribbons are the black sheep because they lack a defining characteristic."

What other black sheep justifications do you see?

DEBRIEF QUESTIONS

To get the most out of this Photo Jolt, ask these questions:

- *Is there value in being able to determine that "one of these things is not like the others?"*
- *How easy or difficult is it to identify a Black Sheep?*
- *What different relationships did your table group identify?*
- *What patterns did you see in how your table members identify relationships?*
- *What does it mean to be a Black Sheep?*

RESOURCES

- *Photo Jolts! Video*: Watch Glenn and Thiagi demonstrate *Black Sheep* and see more *Photo Jolts!* videos at *http://YouTube.com/SMARTasHellVideo*

13

CATEGORIES

How clear or unclear are the categories we create?

We create order in our world through the use of categories: good/bad, male/female, animal/vegetable/mineral. How do we create these categories? And how clear are they?

SYNOPSIS

Participants lay down three random images. They then silently categorize the rest of the deck against these three images. Later they explain how they made their decisions.

PURPOSE

! *Clarity*: Witness the advantages of clear categories.

! *Creativity*: Create a categorization system for random images.

! *Conversation*: Discuss the power of categorization. Discuss best practices for team communication.

TRAINING TOPICS

- *Solo*: How would I categorize these images?
- *One-on-One Coaching*: How would you categorize these images?
- *Communication*: How does communications impact team work?
- *Problem Solving, Decision-making, Critical Thinking*: What strategies do I employ to solve multiple challenges?
- *Science*: How easy is it to create categories in the sciences?
- *Teamwork*: How does your team complete this project?

PARTICIPANTS

- *Minimum*: 1
- *Maximum*: Any number
- *Best*: 3 to 24
- *Configurations*: Solo, Pairs, Triads, or Groups

TIME

- *5 to 15 minutes*: Run in pairs. Limited deck. Short debrief.
- *15 to 30 minutes*: Triads or Groups. Full deck. Deeper debrief.

PREPARATION

- Provide one deck of *Photo Jolts!* cards per 3 participants.
- If you are short on decks, give each team 18 cards and play a shorter version of the activity, or put more players in each team.

- Clear enough table space for three piles or rows of cards.

VIRTUAL FACILITATION OPTIONS (SEE PAGE 21)

✓ Remote Facilitation with Cards

FLOW

1. *Form triads*. Form teams of three.

2. *Distribute decks*. Provide one deck to each triad.

3. *Start silence*. The rest of this exercise is wordless. No talking or writing is allowed.

4. *Seed the categories*. Each team draws three random cards from their deck. Place these cards on the table in front of the team. The categories are determined by these three images

5. *Categorize*. Teams silently sort the rest of the cards into three categories. Allow 5 to 10 minutes for the sort.

6. *End silence.* Teams can talk now. Expect a flurry of conversation.

7. *Align*. Team members discuss how they defined their categories. Allow 5 minutes.

8. *Debrief*. Debrief the activity.

VARIATIONS

- *Wild Card Category*: One time – and one time only – participants can create a new, fourth category. Participants decide (again, silently) when and how to use their wild card.

- *Spoken Categories*: Allow the participants to speak while categorizing their images.

- *Reinforce*: Use this activity to reinforce DISC, MBTI, 5 Dysfunctions of a Team, Tuckman's Team Model, and other team tools.

PLAY SAMPLE

Here is an example using *Photograph 1 – Skyscraper, Photograph 2 – Female Runners, Photograph 3 - Ribbons,* and *Photograph 5 – Umbrella.*

- Three images are dealt: skyscraper, runners, and ribbons.
- Participant 1 sees the categories as architecture, humans, and color.
- Participant 2 sees the categories as shelter, water, and organic.
- Participant 3 sees the categories as vertical, horizontal, and multiples.
- The next image is dealt. It's the red umbrella.

Where might each participant want to categorize the umbrella? What challenges do you foresee the team encountering as they sort through the card deck?

DEBRIEF QUESTIONS

To get the most out of this Photo Jolt, ask these questions:

- *What happened?*
- *What worked or didn't work?*
- *How aligned were your categories?*
- *Were there conflicts? How did you resolve them?*
- *How can you relate this experience to your product (organization, presentation, personal brand, or message)?*
- *Why are categories important?*
- *What happens when we don't agree on categories?*

14

LOTUS BLOSSOM

What do these images have in common?

Invention often consists of the ability to connect items that have never been connected. Can you find a common thread among random items?

SYNOPSIS

Participants articulate a common theme for two random cards. A third card is added and the participant chooses a new theme. This continues until the participant cannot identify a common theme.

PURPOSE

- ! *Clarity*: Identify relationships that link random images.
- ! *Creativity*: See or imagine connections that are not obvious.
- ! *Conversation*: Discuss the importance of meaning and connection.

TRAINING TOPICS

- *Solo*: How can I create meaning?
- *One-on-One Coaching*: Can you create meaning out of random images?
- *Communication*: Can I create meaning out of disparate images (or data or information) for my audience?
- *Design*: What determines relationships? How do color, proximity, content, and context influence perceived relationships?
- *Problem Solving, Decision-making, Critical Thinking*: What level of abstraction allows me to maintain meaningful relationships or categories?

PARTICIPANTS

- † *Minimum*: 1
- † *Maximum*: any number
- † *Best*: 4 to 32
- † *Configurations*: Solo, Pairs, Triads, or Groups

TIME

- ⊕ *< 5 minutes*: Run as described.
- ⊕ *5 to 15 minutes*: Play multiple rounds.

PREPARATION

- Provide one deck of *Photo Jolts!* cards per 2 participants.
- Ask participants to clear table space for this Photo Jolt.

VIRTUAL FACILITATION OPTIONS (SEE PAGE 21)

✓ Image Sharing without Cards
✓ Remote Facilitation with Cards

FLOW

1. *Form pairs*. Each participant finds a partner.

2. *Assign roles*: For each round, one participant is the player while the other participant is the dealer.

3. *Distribute Photo Jolts! decks.* Give each pair a shuffled *Photo Jolts* deck.

4. *Deal image*. The dealer gives one random image to the player.

5. *Identify the theme*. The player identifies a theme for the image. Allow 15 seconds.

6. *Deal another image*. The dealer provides a second random image.

7. *Identify/extend the theme*. The player identifies a theme that unites the two images. The dealer must agree that the relationship exists. Allow 15 seconds.

8. *Deal another image*. The dealer provides a third random image.

9. *Identify/extend the theme*. The player identifies a theme that unites all three images. The deaser must agree that the relationship exists. Allow 15 seconds.

10. *Grow the Lotus Blossom*. Continue adding images and extending the theme until the player cannot identify a unifying theme.

11. *Change roles*. The player now becomes the dealer while the dealer plays.

12. *Debrief.* Debrief the activity.

VARIATIONS

- *Because*: Participant determines a theme for the first photo and then explains how each additional photo extends the theme.
- *Pairs*: Each partner takes turns building the Lotus Blossom. When one player is stuck, the other player can 'steal' their turn and win the game.
- *Theme Tree*: Player one silently selects a theme or topic and then picks a photo aligned with the theme. Player two guesses player one's theme, based on the photo. Player one continues to add photos, while player two continues to guess the theme. The game ends when player two correctly guesses the theme.

PLAY SAMPLE

Here is an example using *Photograph 1 – Skyscraper, Photograph 5 – Umbrella, Photograph 3 – Ribbons, and Photograph 2 – Female Runners.*

- *Dealer deals skyscraper photo*: Participant says, "Towering."
- *Dealer adds umbrella photo*: Participant says, "Shelter."
- *Dealer adds ribbons photo*: Participant says, "Patterns."
- *Dealer adds female runners photo*: Participant says, "I'm stuck. I pass…"

What connection would you make?

DEBRIEF QUESTIONS

To get the most out of this Photo Jolt, ask these questions:

- *What were your strategies?*
- *How is this like designing a presentation, product, or company?*
- *What levels of abstraction did you find most useful?*
- *How do coherent – or incoherent – themes effect communication?*
- *How else does this skill show up in your life or work?*

15
VISUAL MEMORY

How well do you remember details of a photograph?

We use visualization techniques and graphic cues to memorize verbal materials. But how do we remember visual details? How do we memorize a photograph?

SYNOPSIS

Participants study and memorize a photograph. Later they exchange photographs with a partner and quiz each other.

PURPOSE

- ! *Clarity*: Identify the important elements of an image.
- ! *Creativity*: Create statements that stump your partner.
- ! *Conversation*: Explore observation skills and game strategies.

TRAINING TOPICS

- *Observation Skills*: How strong are your observation skills?
- *Problem Solving, Decision-making, Critical Thinking*: Can you develop strategies for winning this game?
- *Psychology (Memory / Brain Training)*: How well can you memorize details quickly?
- *Teamwork*: Should you compete or collaborate?

PARTICIPANTS

- † *Minimum*: 2
- † *Maximum*: Any number
- † *Best*: 10 to 20
- † *Configurations*: Pairs, Triads, or Groups

TIME

- ⏲ *< 5 minutes*: Run as described.
- ⏲ *5 to 15 minutes*: Play multiple rounds.

PREPARATION

- Provide one deck of *Photo Jolts!* cards per 10 participants.
- *ANYWHERE JOLT!* Run this Photo Jolt standing up, in a car, at a desk or table, or virtually.

VIRTUAL FACILITATION OPTIONS (SEE PAGE 21)

- ✓ Image Sharing without Cards
- ✓ Remote Facilitation with Cards

FLOW

1. *Distribute photographs*. Shuffle the deck and give a card to each participant.

2. *Study your photograph*. Study your image, paying attention to details and memorizing as much information as possible. Allow 1 minute.

3. *Find a partner*. Pair up with a partner.

4. *Exchange photographs*. Exchange photographs with your partner.

5. *Quiz each other*. Hold the card so your partner cannot see it. Take turns making a true or false statement related to the card (example: There are parallel lines on the floor). Your partner (who had studied the card earlier) responds "True" or "False." The person holding the card awards one point for each correct answer.

6. *Avoid subjective statements, statements requiring inference, and trivial statements or questions*: Do not pose subjective statements like "The woman is worried about catching pneumonia," statements that require inference like "This is a street in Laos," or trivial questions like "How many leaves are in the bush?" Remind players that 'what goes around comes around'.

7. *Continue the quiz*. Continue until each player has made and responded to five statements. Allow 3 minutes per round.

8. *Switch partners*. At the end of the fifth statement, each participant retrieves their card, thanks their partner, and pairs up with someone else. The game is played in the same fashion until the end of a pre-specified period of time.

9. *Debrief.* Debrief the activity.

VARIATIONS

- *H-O-R-S-E*: Form teams of four. When a participant answers incorrectly or uses the wrong type of question, assign one letter of the word 'HORSE' to the participant. When a participant spells the word 'HORSE', he or she is ejected from the game. Continue until one player remains. Shorten this game by playing F-A-I-L or B-A-D.

- *Reverse or 'Turnabout is Fair Play'*: If the questioner poses a statement or question that is not knowable, the respondent can reverse that question by saying, "I don't know. What is the correct answer?" If the questioner cannot answer, the respondent gains a point.

- *3D Visual Memory*: Play *Visual Memory* with three cards per participant. Each player will memorize the three cards and then be quizzed by their partner on all three cards. For example, "True or False? In these three cards, there are five people."

PLAY SAMPLES

Here are five statements about *Photograph 2 – Female Runners*.

- All taxis in the photo are yellow.
- There are two taxis.
- Two people are drenched in the rain.
- The name of the road is "Paterson Road."
- You can see a red traffic light.

Would you correctly respond to these statements?

What other statements would you make?

DEBRIEF QUESTIONS

To get the most out of this Photo Jolt, ask these questions:

- *How good is your memory?*
- *What memorization strategies did you use? What questioning strategies did you use?*
- *What strategies worked?*
- *Did you get better as the game went on? Why or why not?*
- *Did you consider collaborating instead of competing? If so, how did you collaborate?*

RESOURCES

- ☛ ***Photo Jolts! Video***: Watch Glenn and Thiagi demonstrate *Visual Memory* and see more *Photo Jolts!* videos at *http://YouTube.com/SMARTasHellVideo*

16
INSERT AND REMOVE

How good is your visual memory?

Our memory uses visuals for storage. This card game challenges the participants to remember a set of photographs.

SYNOPSIS

Participants study and memorize a set of photographs. Later they identify an extra photograph (one they had not seen before) and a missing photograph.

PURPOSE

! *Clarity*: Identify changes in a complex environment.

! *Creativity*: Create memory-enhancing strategies.

! *Conversation*: Discuss winning game strategies.

TRAINING TOPICS

- *Observation Skills*: How strong are your observation skills?

- *Problem Solving, Decision-making, Critical Thinking*: Can you develop strategies for winning this game?

- *Psychology (Memory / Brain Training)*: How well you can memorize details quickly?

- *Teamwork*: How can your team work together to win?

PARTICIPANTS

- *Minimum*: 2

- *Maximum*: 28

- *Best*: 2 to 7 per group

- *Configurations*: Groups

TIME

- *< 5 minutes*: One round. Short debrief.

- *5 to 15 minutes*: Multiple rounds. Full debrief.

PREPARATION

- Provide one deck of *Photo Jolts!* cards per table group.

- Ask participants to clear table space for this Photo Jolt.

VIRTUAL FACILITATION OPTIONS (SEE PAGE 21)

✓ Remote Facilitation with Cards

FLOW

1. *Form teams*. Form teams of four to five players at each table.

2. *Choose a dealer*. Select one participant at each table to be the dealer. Everyone takes a turn as dealer during the subsequent rounds.

3. *Deal nine photographs*. The dealer shuffles the deck of cards and deals the top nine cards, *photo side up*, in the middle of the table.

4. *Deal tenth photograph*. The dealer privately looks at the photo on the tenth card, memorizes this photo, and then places the card *photo side down* at a suitable location on the table. Set the rest of the deck aside.

5. *Memorize photos*. Participants memorize the nine photos. Allow 30 seconds.

6. *Insert the tenth card*. The dealer collect the nine cards from the table and turns the packet photo side down. The dealer inserts the tenth card and shuffles the packet thoroughly.

7. *Slap the new card*. The dealer places the 10 cards on the table, one at a time, *photo side up*. The participants watch these cards and slap the image they have not seen before. The first person to slap the correct image card (cover the card with her hand) wins a point. If the participant slaps an incorrect card, the dealer says, "Wrong." This participant is not permitted to slap a card during the rest of this round. The dealer continues placing the remaining cards from the packet while the other participants race to slap the new card.

8. *Remove a card*. After the newly inserted image is correctly identified, the dealer picks up the 10 cards and shuffles the packet. The dealer removes the top card from the packet and, without showing the photo on the card to anyone, places it aside. The dealer then spreads the other nine cards, *photo side up*, on the table.

9. *Identify the missing card*. Participants guess which card is missing. The first player to raise a hand gets to describe the photo on the missing card. The dealer picks up the tenth card and decides if the player's description is correct. This player gets a point for correctly identifying the missing card.

10. *Continue the game*. The dealer adds the ten cards to the rest of the deck and passes it to the next player, who becomes the new dealer. Repeat the game until everyone has played the role of dealer.

11. *Debrief*. Debrief the activity.

VARIATIONS

- *Raise the Bar*: Add an extra card for each round (9 cards in the first round, 10 cards in the second round, 11 cards in the third round, and so on...) until every player has played the role of the dealer, or until the team fails to finish a round.

- *Insert-a-Card*: Play only steps 1 through 4 of Insert and Remove.

- *Remove-a-Card*: Skip steps 3 and 4 of Insert and Remove.

DEBRIEF QUESTIONS

To get the most out of this Photo Jolt, ask these questions:

- *What strategies did you apply?*
- *What strategies worked or didn't work?*
- *How is this game like your workplace (competitive, increasing workload, small details are important in a complex environment)?*
- *What are the ramifications of this environment?*
- *Did you work together as a team? How could you use teamwork to win this game?*

17
ETHNOGRAPHER

What can you tell about a culture from a photo?

When exposed to new cultures, we are required to make judgments based on small samples of information. How well does that work?

SYNOPSIS

Participants study a random photograph. They then act as ethnographers and make educated guesses about the culture contained in that scene.

PURPOSE

! *Clarity*: Learn about culture from fellow participants.

! *Creativity*: Imagine a culture, based on one photo.

! *Conversation*: Discuss critical thinking and aspects of culture.

TRAINING TOPICS

- *Solo*: How skilled am I at observation and interpretation?
- *One-on-One Coaching*: How skilled are you at observation and interpretation?
- *Culture, Diversity, Perspective*: What do these artifacts say about the culture that produced them? How can we compare and contrast artifacts from different photos?
- *Observation Skills*: What do I see in this photo?
- *Problem Solving, Decision-making, Critical Thinking*: What conclusions can we draw from what we see in this photo?

PARTICIPANTS

- *Minimum*: 1
- *Maximum*: any number
- *Best*: 4 to 20
- *Configurations*: Triads or Groups

TIME

- *5 to 15 minutes*: One round. Short debrief.
- *15 to 30 minutes*: Multiple rounds. Full debrief.
- *30 to 60 minutes*: Combine with *Naturalist, Soundtrack,* or *Deeper* for longer play.

PREPARATION

- Provide one deck of *Photo Jolts!* cards for up to 40 participants.
- Pre-select the roughly 40 images that contain human artifacts. Remove the other images.
- Provide one *Ethnographer Worksheet* for each team.

VIRTUAL FACILITATION OPTIONS (SEE PAGE 21)

- ✓ Image Sharing without Cards
- ✓ Video Sharing with Cards
- ✓ Audio Sharing with Cards
- ✓ Remote Facilitation with Cards

FLOW

1. *Form pairs or teams*. Form pairs or teams.
2. *Distribute photographs*. Each pair or team receives a random image.
3. *<Optional> Identify 'guides'*. Identify anyone at the table who is familiar with the culture contained in the photograph. Ask them to observe the activity. Later, they will act as guides. Alternatively, choose a card that the table is unfamiliar with.
4. *Be ethnographers*. Announce, "Your image documents a culture identified only as 'the Unknowns'. Your team will identify artifacts in the image that provide clues about 'the Unknowns'. Your team will then draw conclusions about 'the Unknowns' culture based on these clues." Each team must identify at least five conclusions. Allow 5 minutes.
5. *Determine confidence*. Discuss your team's confidence level for each of your conclusions. Allow 3 minutes.

6. *<Optional> Feedback.* Guides now provide feedback on the conclusions. Allow 3 minutes.

7. *Debrief.* Debrief the activity.

VARIATIONS

- *Two-Card Culture*: Choose two cards and identify similarities and differences between the cultures.

- *Customer Culture*: Select an image that best represents your customer's culture. How will you join and thrive in this culture?

- *Combine with Naturalist, Soundtrack, Deeper*: Combine *Ethnographer* with these *Photo Jolts!* for longer play and deeper discussion.

PLAY SAMPLE

Here is an example using *Photograph 1 – Skyscraper.*

- In the image, a team identifies a skyscraper, steel, glass, and the color gray. They then draw the following conclusions:

- This culture honors the sky.

- This culture does not fear heights.

- This culture does not value color.

- This culture is technologically developed.

- This culture uses levels to create status.

What other statements would you make?

How much confidence do you have in their conclusions?

DEBRIEF QUESTIONS

To get the most out of this Photo Jolt, ask these questions:

- *How easy or difficult was this exercise?*

- *Were there disagreements? How did you settle them?*

- *How much confidence did you have in your conclusions?*

- *How would you increase your confidence?*

- *What did the observers note?*

- *What is the culture of your team, organization, or environment?*

- *What is the culture of your customer?*

- *How can you better adapt to, or survive your customer' culture?*

RESOURCES

- ☞ *Ethnographer Worksheet*: Download *Photo Jolts!* worksheets from *http://PhotoJolts.com*

ETHNOGRAPHER WORKSHEET

What artifacts do I see in this image?

1.

2.

3.

4.

5.

What conclusions can I draw about this culture from the artifacts?

1.

2.

3.

4.

5.

How much confidence do I have in these conclusions?

18
NATURALIST

What can you tell about your surroundings from a photo?

When exposed to new environments we are required to make judgments based on small samples of information. How well does that work?

SYNOPSIS

Participants study a random photograph. They then assess the environment based on the information contained in that scene.

PURPOSE

- *Clarity*: Learn about unfamiliar environments from fellow participants.
- *Creativity*: Imagine an environment, based on one photo.
- *Conversation*: Discuss critical thinking and aspects of the natural world.

TRAINING TOPICS

- *Solo*: How strong are my observation and interpretation skills?
- *One-on-One Coaching*: How strong are your observation and interpretation skills?
- *Business*: How can we adapt to and survive our environment?
- *Culture, Diversity, Perspective*: How can we compare and contrast clues from different photos?
- *Science / Nature*: What do these clues say about the natural environment that produced them?
- *Observation Skills*: What do I see in this photo?
- *Problem Solving, Decision-making, Critical Thinking*: What conclusions can we draw from what we see in this photo?
- *Training (Workplace or School Orientation)*: What strategies enable me to survive and thrive in this new school, workplace, or other environment?

PARTICIPANTS

- *Minimum*: 1
- *Maximum*: any number
- *Best*: 4 to 20
- *Configurations*: Triads or Groups

TIME

- 🕐 *5 to 15 minutes*: One round. Short debrief.
- 🕐 *15 to 30 minutes*: Multiple rounds. Full debrief.

PREPARATION

- Provide one deck of *Photo Jolts!* cards per 8 participants.
- Pre-select the roughly 25 images that contain natural elements. Remove the 'unnatural' images. Alternatively, you can increase your number of natural images by purchasing the *Nature Jolts!* activity cards or the *Animal Jolts!* activity cards from *http://PhotoJolts.com*
- Provide one *Naturalist Worksheet* for each team.
- *ANYWHERE JOLT!* Run this Photo Jolt standing up, in a car, at a desk or table, or virtually.

VIRTUAL FACILITATION OPTIONS (SEE PAGE 21)

- ✓ Image Sharing without Cards
- ✓ Video Sharing with Cards
- ✓ Audio Sharing with Cards
- ✓ Remote Facilitation with Cards

FLOW

1. *Form pairs or teams*. Form pairs or teams.
2. *Distribute photographs*. Each pair or team receives a random image.
3. *<Optional> Identify 'guides'*. Identify participants who are knowledgeable about the natural environment contained in the photograph. Ask them to observe the activity. Later, they will act

as guides. Alternatively, choose a card that the table is unfamiliar with.

4. *Be naturalists*. Announce, "Your image documents a natural environment identified only as 'the Unknown'. Your team will identify elements in the image that provide clues about 'the Unknown'. Your team will then draw conclusions about 'the Unknown' environment based on these clues." Each team must identify at least five conclusions. Allow 5 minutes.

5. *Determine confidence*. Discuss your team's confidence level for each of your conclusions. Allow 3 minutes.

6. *<Optional> Feedback*. Guides now provide feedback on the conclusions. Allow 3 minutes.

7. *Debrief*. Debrief the activity.

VARIATIONS

- *Two-card Environment*: Choose two cards and identify similarities and differences between the environments.

- *Customer Environment*: Select an image that best represents your customer's environment. How will you survive or even thrive in this environment?

- *Combine with Ethnographer, Soundtrack, Textures, Deeper*: Combine *Naturalist* with these *Photo Jolts!* for longer play and deeper discussion.

PLAY SAMPLE

Here is an example using *Photograph 2 – Female Runners*.

From exploring this photo, a team drew the following conclusions about the environment:

- The environment is warm (one woman is wearing few clothes).
- Rain occurs suddenly (the women seem unprepared).
- It is a mature natural environment (the trees are big).
- It is a summer-like season (the trees have leaves).
- It is not windy (the rain is falling straight down).
- It is daytime.

What other statements would you make?

DEBRIEF QUESTIONS

To get the most out of this Photo Jolt, ask these questions:

- *How easy or difficult was this exercise?*
- *Where there disagreements? How did you settle them?*
- *How much confidence did you have in your conclusions?*
- *How would you increase your confidence?*
- *What did the observers note?*
- *What is the environment your team, organization, or product exists in?*
- *What is the environment of your customer?*
- *How can you better adapt to, or survive your environment?*

RESOURCES

- ☛ *Naturalist Worksheet*: Download *Photo Jolts!* worksheets from *http://PhotoJolts.com*

NATURALIST WORKSHEET

What clues do I see in this image?

1.

2.

3.

4.

5.

What conclusions can I draw about this culture from the clues?

1.

2.

3.

4.

5.

How much confidence do I have in these conclusions?

19
SOUNDTRACK

Can you communicate a scene using no words or images?

Our environment is full of sounds, but how well do we listen to the world around us? How able are we to describe or convey those sounds to others?

SYNOPSIS

Participants study a photograph and identify sounds in the photo. Later they share the sounds in the photograph with fellow participants.

PURPOSE

- ! *Clarity*: Accurately describe a soundscape.
- ! *Creativity*: Imagine the soundscape of an image.
- ! *Conversation*: Practice unusual methods of communication.

TRAINING TOPICS

- *Solo*: How strong are my observation and communication skills?
- *One-on-One Coaching*: How strong are your observation and communication skills?
- *Communication*: How closely do I listen to my environment? How can we communicate a scene through non-verbal sounds?
- *Creativity*: How can we recreate the sounds of this environment?
- *Culture, Diversity, Perspective*: How do different people hear their environment?
- *Design*: How can I use sound on my product or project?
- *Teamwork*: How well can I work with my team to reach this goal?

PARTICIPANTS

- *Minimum*: 1
- *Maximum*: any number
- *Best*: 8 to 24
- *Configurations*: Solo, Pairs, Triads, or Groups

TIME

- *5 to 15 minutes*: Run one round in pairs or triads. Debrief.
- *15 to 30 minutes*: Run multiple rounds in groups. Debrief.

PREPARATION

- Provide one deck of *Photo Jolts!* cards for up to 50 participants.

- *ANYWHERE JOLT!* Run this Photo Jolt standing up, in a car, at a desk or table, or virtually.

- <Optional> A facilitator can make this Photo Jolt more or less challenging by pre-sorting the cards and eliminating (or focusing on) cards with obvious sounds.

VIRTUAL FACILITATION OPTIONS (SEE PAGE 21)

- ✓ Image Sharing without Cards
- ✓ Video Sharing with Cards
- ✓ Audio Sharing with Cards
- ✓ Remote Facilitation with Cards

FLOW

1. *Choose photographs*. Choose an image that resonates with you.

2. *Imagine the soundtrack*. If this were a movie, what would the soundtrack be? Clarify that 'soundtrack' does not mean 'music' (unless you play the *Photo Jolts! Musical* variation below).

3. *Explore the image for possible sounds*. Identify sounds that are not literal. The participant cannot say, for example, "It sounds like a building." They might, however, say, "I hear the voices of office workers entering the building." Allow 3 minutes.

4. *Share the literal sound descriptions*. Share your soundtrack with a partner or table group. Allow 1 minute per participant.

5. *Make the sounds*. Mimic the sounds in the scene. Allow 1 minute per participant.

6. *Add more sounds*. Partners (or table groups) now add other sounds that they can identify in the image. Allow 1 minute per participant.

7. *Debrief*. Debrief the activity.

VARIATIONS

- *Family Fight*: Form three teams of two to four participants. Team one is the audience. They list the sounds they see in the photo. Teams two and three then guess which sounds the audience identified. The team that gets the most right wins!

- *Randomize*: Do not allow the participants to choose their own photos. Instead, have them select from the deck randomly.

- *Soundtrack Game*: Do not share the image or describe the sounds. Instead, mimic the sounds in the photo and ask your partner or tablemates to guess the image.

- *Team Soundtrack Game*: Form two teams of three to four participants. One member communicates an image to his or her teammates, using only sounds. The team that identifies the most images correctly wins.

- *Orchestra*: A group of three to four participants communicates a photo to the larger room by layering sounds where appropriate.

- *Musical*: What would the musical soundtrack for this scene be? Classical? Jazz? Rock? Ethnic? What song? Can you sing or hum it?

- *Combine with Ethnographer, Naturalist, Textures, Deeper*: Combine *Soundtrack* with these *Photo Jolts!* for longer play and deeper discussion.

PLAY SAMPLE

Here is an example using *Photograph 1 – Skyscraper*.

- *Participant 1*: "I hear wind whipping around the building."
- *Participant 2*: "I hear the footsteps of office workers leaving the building."
- *Participant 3*: "I hear horns and automobile traffic on the busy streets around the building."

What other sounds can you imagine?

How would you mimic these sounds?

DEBRIEF QUESTIONS

To get the most out of this Photo Jolt, ask these questions:

- *How easy or difficult is it to identify sounds in the image?*
- *How easy or difficult is it to describe those sounds?*
- *How easy or difficult is it to mimic those sounds?*
- *What is the 'soundtrack' of your team, environment, or current challenge? Is it quiet, cacophonous, or melodic? Discuss in your group.*
- *What should your product or environment sound like?*

20
TEXTURES

How vivid is your tactile memory?

Our world is full of textures. But how much attention do we pay to them? How able are we to describe those textures to others?

SYNOPSIS

Participants choose a photograph. Later they describe the textures that they imagine in the scene.

PURPOSE

- ! *Clarity*: Accurately describe textures.
- ! *Creativity*: Imagine the textures in an image.
- ! *Conversation*: Communicate in the language of textures.

TRAINING TOPICS

- *Solo*: How strong are my observation skills?
- *One-on-One Coaching*: How strong are your observation skills?
- *Communication*: How can we communicate the way a scene feels?
- *Creativity*: How can we describe the textures in this environment?
- *Culture, Diversity, Perspective*: How do different people 'feel' their environment?
- *Design*: How can I use textures on my product or project?
- *Teamwork*: How well can I work with my team to reach this goal?

PARTICIPANTS

- *Minimum*: 1
- *Maximum*: any number
- *Best*: 8 to 24
- *Configurations*: Solo, Pairs, Triads, or Groups

TIME

- < *5 minutes*: Run one round in pairs or triads. Debrief.
- *5 to 15 minutes*: Run multiple rounds in pairs or triads. Debrief.

PREPARATION

- Provide one deck of *Photo Jolts!* cards per 12 participants.
- *ANYWHERE JOLT!* Run this Photo Jolt standing up, in a car, at a desk or table, or virtually.

- <Optional> A facilitator can make this Photo Jolt more or less challenging by pre-sorting the cards and eliminating (or focusing on) cards with obvious textures.

VIRTUAL FACILITATION OPTIONS (SEE PAGE 21)

- ✓ Image Sharing without Cards
- ✓ Video Sharing with Cards
- ✓ Audio Sharing with Cards
- ✓ Remote Facilitation with Cards

FLOW

1. *Choose photographs.* Participants choose an image that resonates with them. Allow 1 to 2 minutes.

2. *Identify textures.* "If you were blindfolded, what textures would you feel in this scene?"

3. *Explore the image for textures.* Identify textures that are not literal. The participant cannot say, for example, "It feels like a building." They might say, however, "I feel the coldness of metal." Allow 2 to 3 minutes.

4. *Share the textures.* Share your findings with a partner or table group. Allow 1 minute.

5. *Add more textures.* Add other textures you can identify in the image. Allow 1 to 2 minutes.

6. **Debrief.** Debrief the activity.

VARIATIONS

- *Family Fight*: Bring together three teams of two to three people. Team one is the audience. They list the textures they see in the photo. Teams two and three then try to guess which textures the audience identified. The team that gets the most right wins!

- *Randomize*: Do not allow the participants to choose their own photos. Instead, have them select from the deck randomly.

- *Team 'Textures' Game*: Form two teams of three to four people. Given an image, one member communicates that image to his or her teammates, using only textures. The team that identifies the most images correctly wins.

- *Simulator*: Can you share the textures and feelings with your colleagues without words? How would you do that? This exercise is worth a discussion, even if you don't play it.

- *Scratch-n-Sniff*: Use the same format as Soundtrack or Textures, but identify scents that are present in an image; "I smell dampness in the air, cold metal, and the sting of pollution."

- *Combine with Ethnographer, Naturalist, Soundtrack, Deeper*: Combine *Soundtrack* with these *Photo Jolts!* for longer play and deeper discussion.

PLAY SAMPLE

Here is an example using *Photograph 1 – Skyscraper*.

- *Participant 1*: "I feel dampness in the air, from the fog."
- *Participant 2*: "I feel cold metal."
- *Participant 3*: "I feel vibrations from motors nearby."

What other textures can you identify?

DEBRIEF QUESTIONS

To get the most out of this Photo Jolt, ask these questions:

- *How easy or difficult is it to identify textures in the image?*
- *How easy or difficult is it to describe those textures?*
- *What is the 'texture' of your team, environment, product, or current challenge? Is it silky, rough, or rubbery? Discuss in your group.*
- *What should your product, environment, or challenge feel like?*

21
DEEPER

How deep are your skills of observation?

We can look at a scene hundreds of times without noticing an obvious detail. How much detail can we find in an image if we look deeper?

SYNOPSIS

Participants form pairs or triads and identify as many details as possible in an image.

PURPOSE

- ! *Clarity*: Look deeper into an image or environment.
- ! *Creativity*: Imagine what's 'unseen in a scene'.
- ! *Conversation*: Discuss how easy it is to overlook details in our environment.

TRAINING TOPICS

- *Solo*: What details can I find in this image?
- *One-on-One Coaching*: What details can you find in this image?
- *Communication*: What are others seeing that I am not?
- *Design*: How important are details to a design?
- *Problem Solving, Decision-making, Critical Thinking*: How can I develop my observation skills?
- *Sales and Marketing*: What am I communicating visually?

PARTICIPANTS

- *Minimum*: 1
- *Maximum*: Any number
- *Best*: 3 to 30
- *Configurations*: Pairs, Triads, or Groups

TIME

- *< 5 minutes*: Run in pairs. Short debrief.
- *5 to 15 minutes*: Run in triads. Multiple rounds. Full debrief.
- *15 minutes or more*: Combine with other *Photo Jolts!* for deeper reflection, debate, and exploration (see *Variations* below).

PREPARATION

- Provide one deck of *Photo Jolts!* cards for up to 50 participants.
- *ANYWHERE JOLT!* Run this Photo Jolt standing up, in a car, at a desk or table, or virtually.

VIRTUAL FACILITATION OPTIONS (SEE PAGE 21)

✓ Image Sharing without Cards
✓ Video Sharing with Cards
✓ Remote Facilitation with Cards

FLOW

1. *Form teams.* Form pairs, triads, or teams.
2. *Distribute photographs.* Shuffle the deck and give a card to each pair, triad, or team.
3. *Identify a detail in the image.* Player one names an object or detail in the image.
4. *Identify another detail.* Player two names another object or detail. Synonyms are not allowed.
5. *Go deeper into the image.* Continue identifying details until you cannot. How far can you go?
6. *Continue.* Distribute a new image. Play three rounds or until time expires.
7. *Debrief.* Debrief the activity.

VARIATIONS

- *Easter Egg Hunt*: Players list the details in a random image. Give each player a point for noticing something that no one else noticed. Take away a point if something they noticed didn't exist. Who wins?

- *Gamification*: If a player is stumped, they are disqualified. The last player to identify details is declared the winner.

- *Likely, Possible, or Fantasy*: A participant imagines what else is in the scene. Other participants then classify the suggestion as likely, possible, or fantasy. Play one round focusing on likely suggestions, one round focusing on possibilities, and one round focusing on fantasy. Which is most difficult for you?

- *Synonyms*: In this version, synonyms are allowed. It makes the game longer, but serves as great vocabulary practice.

- *Team Identification*: In this variation, the team works together. One member might point at a detail and ask, "What is this thing called?" while another responds, "That's a cornice." Count how many details you can name. Optionally, allow players to use the Internet to identify or confirm names.

- *Unseen Scene*: Imagine what unseen objects are in the scene. Are there fleas on the dog? Are there stars in the sky? Are there desks or elevators in the skyscraper?

- *God is in the Details*: Choose a minor detail in the photo and explain why it is the most important thing in the photo. Your partner then picks another detail and explains why it is more important. Continue until a player surrenders or a third-party judge declares a winner.

- *Combine with Ethnographer, Naturalist, Textures, Soundtrack*: Combine *Deeper* with these *Photo Jolts!* for longer play and deeper discussion.

PLAY SAMPLE

Here is an example using *Photograph 1 - Skyscraper*.

- *Player 1 says,* "I see a skyscraper."
- *Player 2 says,* "I see mist."
- *Player 1 says,* "I see windows."
- *Player 2 says,* "I see lights inside some windows."
- *Player 1 says,* "I see a light coming from the top of the skyscraper."

How much deeper can you go?

DEBRIEFING

To get the most out of this Photo Jolt, ask these questions:

- *How important are details?*
- *When is the ability to recognize details important?*
- *How does previous experience help your ability to identify details? If you are an architect, will you see more details in a building? Are you better able to articulate those details?*
- *What causes 'blind spots'?*
- *What strategies or methods did you use to identify details?*

Looking for a metaphor

RESOURCES

- *Invisible Gorilla Video*: Learn more about selective attention by viewing this video at *http://theinvisiblegorilla.com/videos.html*

22
NOTICE

What do you notice first - or not at all?

We assume that we all see the same thing when we look at the same thing. Let's test that assumption, shall we?

SYNOPSIS

Participants write down three things they notice about a random picture. How are their observations similar or different?

PURPOSE

! *Clarity*: Align on what we see in an image.

! *Creativity*: Determine whether you see differently than others.

! *Conversation*: Discuss the difference between looking and seeing. Discuss differences in what we notice.

TRAINING TOPICS

- *Solo*: What do I notice?
- *One-on-One Coaching*: What do you notice or not notice?
- *Culture, Diversity, Perspective*: Do we see differently? If so, why?
- *Design*: What do people notice? Why? Can I design a visual that creates consistent reactions among different people?
- *Observation Skills*: What can I see that others overlook?

PARTICIPANTS

- *Minimum*: 2
- *Maximum*: any number
- *Best*: 4 to 32
- *Configuration*: Groups

TIME

- *< 5 minutes*: One round. Short debrief.
- *5 to 15 minutes*: Multiple rounds. Full debrief.
- *15 minutes or more*: Combine with other *Photo Jolts!* to allow more complex experiences and deeper debriefs.

PREPARATION

- Provide one deck of *Photo Jolts!* cards per 12 participants.
- Provide one *Notice Worksheet* for each participant.

- Provide one pencil or pen for each participant
- Ask participants to clear table space for this Photo Jolt.

VIRTUAL FACILITATION OPTIONS (SEE PAGE 21)

✓ Image Sharing without Cards
✓ Remote Facilitation with Cards

FLOW

1. *Form teams*. Form teams of three to five participants.
2. *Distribute photographs*. Deal each team a random image. Place the image face down.
3. *Set time*. Participants have 30 seconds for the next action.
4. *View image*. Turn over the image (face up) and memorize it. Allow 30 seconds.
5. *Close image*. Turn the image back over (face down).
6. *What did you notice?* List the first three things you noticed about the image – if you noticed three things. Allow 30 seconds.
7. *What else?* List everything else you saw in the image. Allow another 30 seconds.
8. *Share*. Share your findings with your teammates.
9. *Review Photo*. Look at the photo to confirm your findings.
10. *Debrief*. Debrief the activity.

VARIATIONS

- *Only I See*: Give each player a point for anything they noticed that no one else noticed. Take away a point for anything they noticed that didn't exist. Who wins?

- *Why Do You See That?* Ask why your partner notices certain things. Is there a pattern to what they notice? How can we leverage these patterns?

- *Combine with Deeper*: Continue this exercise with *Photo Jolt #21 - Deeper*.

PLAY SAMPLE

Here is an example using *Photograph 1 - Skyscraper*.

- *Participant 1 says*, "I noticed the tower, the many windows, and that the building was tilted."

- *Participant 2 says*, "I noticed the tilt first, then the lights in the windows, and the fog at the top."

- *Participant 3 says*, "I noticed the tower, the windows, and the light on top."
- *Participant 1 says*, "I also saw sharp edges. That's all."
- *Participant 2 says*, "I thought it looked art deco. I saw the light on top. I also noticed what looks like the elevator shaft in the middle."
- *Participant 3 says*, "Wow... I didn't really notice anything else."

What do you notice?

DEBRIEF QUESTIONS

To get the most out of this Photo Jolt, ask these questions:

- *Did you all notice the same 'first three' in the same order?*
- *Did you all notice the same things? Why or why not?*
- *What did some see that others didn't? Why?*
- *Were some of you looking for certain details? Why?*
- *Is noticing a skill?*
- *Did you see anything that wasn't there? Why?*
- *Which types of images create more alignment?*
- *Which types of images create less alignment?*
- *What does this suggest about the images we use in advertising or presentations?*

RESOURCES

- *Notice Worksheet*: Download *Photo Jolts!* worksheets from *http://PhotoJolts.com*

NOTICE WORKSHEET

List the first three things you notice in this image?

     1.

     2.

     3.

Did you notice anything else in the time allotted?

-

-

-

-

Why did you notice what you noticed?

-

-

-

-

23
CLUES

What can you deduce from this evidence?

We can learn about a person from the evidence in their office or home. What can you learn from these photographs?

SYNOPSIS

Participants see three images from a person's office or home. They then draw conclusions about the person from the images.

PURPOSE

! *Clarity*: Gain insights into a person of interest.

! *Creativity*: Imagine what images might explain about a person you are interested in.

! *Conversation*: Discuss what we can learn about someone from limited evidence.

TRAINING TOPICS

- *Solo*: How strong are my powers of observation and deduction?

- *One-on-One Coaching*: How strong are your powers of observation and deduction?

- *Observation Skills*: How strong are our powers of observation and deduction?

- *Sales and Marketing*: How would you tailor your messaging to appeal to the person who owns these images?

- *Training*: What can you learn about your target audience from the images they collect?

PARTICIPANTS

† *Minimum*: 1

† *Maximum*: any number

† *Best*: 4 to 32

† *Configurations*: Solo, Pairs, Triads, or Groups

TIME

🕐 *5 to 15 minutes*: One round. Short debrief.

🕐 *15 to 30 minutes*: Two rounds. Deep debrief.

🕐 *30 to 60 minutes*: Three or more rounds. Deep debrief.

PREPARATION

- Provide one deck of *Photo Jolts!* cards per 12 participants.
- Provide one *Clues Worksheet* for each team.

VIRTUAL FACILITATION OPTIONS (SEE PAGE 21)

- ✓ Image Sharing without Cards
- ✓ Video Sharing with Cards
- ✓ Audio Sharing with Cards
- ✓ Remote Facilitation with Cards

FLOW

1. *Set the stage*. You are visiting a customer you have never met. The secretary seats you in the customer's office, serves you a drink, and asks you to relax and wait for 15 minutes. You can't help but notice three photographs on the customer's wall. The secretary tells you that the customer picked those photographs personally.

2. *Distribute photographs*. Deal each participant or team three random images.

3. *Look for clues*. Look for clues about the customer, based on the photos in their office. What assumptions would you make about the customer? Allow 5 minutes.

4. *Identify 'bridges'*. Based on the images, might you have anything in common with this customer? Allow 3 minutes.

5. *Create strategies*. Based on the images, what approaches are you considering for this customer? Allow 3 minutes.

6. *Share*. Ask the participants to share their thoughts and strategies with the other participants. Allow 2 minutes per participant.

7. *Debrief*. Debrief the activity.

VARIATIONS

- *Criminal Justice*: You are tracking a criminal. These photos are in the criminal's wallet. How could you use this evidence?

- *First Date*: You're on a first date. You meet your date at their apartment, where these photos are hanging. What are your thoughts, feelings, and questions?

- *New Intern*: Your eccentric boss doesn't like interviews or resumes. He wants you to choose your next intern based on photos they sent in. He gives you three photos that the top three candidates sent to express their work style. Which do you choose and why?

- *Clues Fiesta*: Combine *Clues*, *Criminal Justice*, *First Date*, and *New Intern* by splitting your participants into four groups. Have each group complete a different *Clues* challenge and then present back to the room. How did the approaches and findings differ?

- *Environment*: Picture your manager's office (or another office you know well). Describe or draw it for your partner. Have your partner assess and build a strategy for approaching your manager. Confirm if their approach is reasonable. Use this activity to reinforce DISC, MBTI, or other personality assessments.

- *Real Clues*: Take a photo of a real office. Assess and build a strategy for approaching the person who works in this office. Confirm if their approach is reasonable. Use this activity to reinforce DISC, MBTI, or other personality assessments.

PLAY SAMPLE

Here is an example using *Photograph 1 - Skyscraper, Photograph 2 – Female Runners*, and *Photograph 3 – Ribbons*.

Assumptions made by the participant:

- The customer likes strong imagery, based on the skyscraper and ribbon photos.
- The runner photo is not typical of a store-bought photo, so the customer or someone they knew probably took these photos.
- The runners are someone they know.
- One of the runners might be the customer.
- The customer is a runner.
- The customer probably has traveled to Asia.
- The customer might like architecture.

Common threads:

- I've been to Asia and I like to run.

Strategy:

- Ask the customer, "Do you run?"

What other assumptions and strategies would you consider?

DEBRIEF QUESTIONS

To get the most out of this Photo Jolt, ask these questions:

- *How easy or difficult was it to make assumptions?*
- *Are assumptions useful?*
- *What is the danger in making assumptions?*
- *Do your assumptions say more about them or you? How? Why?*
- *Have you made correct assumptions in the past? How often?*
- *What common strategies did we surface?*

RESOURCES

- **Clues Worksheet**: Download *Photo Jolts!* worksheets from *http://PhotoJolts.com*

CLUES WORKSHEET

What is in Image 1?

What assumptions might you make from this image?

What is in Image 2?

What assumptions might you make from this image?

What is in Image 3?

What assumptions might you make from this image?

What common ground or 'bridges' can you find?

1.
2.
3.

What actions or strategies could you use?

1.
2.
3.

24

SUNNY MONKEY

Can your situation be 'Sunny as a Monkey'?

Similes are a great tool for brainstorming. Is your organization or product 'Hungry like a Wolf'? Unfortunately, many similes have become clichés. How can we generate and apply new, useful similes?

SYNOPSIS

Participants select two random cards. They describe one with an adjective and the other with a noun. They then create a simile with the two words and generate ideas for their situation or topic.

PURPOSE

! *Clarity*: Remove preconceptions about your topic or situation.

! *Creativity*: Generate solutions through the use of similes and metaphors.

! *Conversation*: Discuss the use of similes. Provoke alternative viewpoints on common subjects.

TRAINING TOPICS

- *Solo*: Can I use similes to stimulate new ideas and approaches?
- *One-on-One Coaching*: Can you use similes to stimulate new ideas and approaches?
- *Communication*: What is a simile? Where does a simile come from? How do different cultures view similes?
- *Creativity*: How is my product, situation, or topic *Sunny like a Monkey*?
- *Sales and Marketing*: How can I generate new features and benefits that resonate with my audience?
- *Training*: How can I help participants personalize and retain what they've learned?

PARTICIPANTS

† *Minimum*: 1
† *Maximum*: any number
† *Best*: 4 to 32
† *Configurations*: Solo, Pairs, Triads, or Groups

TIME

🕐 *< 5 minutes*: One round in teams. Short debrief.
🕐 *5 to 15 minutes*: One round in teams. Full debrief.

🕐 *15 to 30 minutes*: Run in teams. Multiple rounds. Full debrief.

🕐 *30 to 60 minutes*: Run in pairs. Multiple rounds. Deep debrief.

PREPARATION

- Provide one deck of *Photo Jolts!* cards per 12 participants.

- Spread out the *Photo Jolts!* images on an open table or surface.

- *ANYWHERE JOLT!* Run this Photo Jolt standing up, in a car, at a desk or table, or virtually.

VIRTUAL FACILITATION OPTIONS (SEE PAGE 21)

✓ Image Sharing without Cards

✓ Video Sharing with Cards

✓ Audio Sharing with Cards

✓ Remote Facilitation with Cards

FLOW

1. *<Optional> Explain Similes.* Provide a description of similes, with examples. Complete the following similes: "As 'what' as ice", "As 'what' as a feather", "As 'what' as a bee", "As 'what' as a bug in a rug?" (Answers: cold, light, busy, snug)

2. *Define the situation or topic.* Introduce participants to the situation or topic of your meeting, workshop, or event (see *Table A* for possible topics).

3. *Distribute photographs.* Hand two random images to each participant or team.

4. *Use one image as the adjective.* State an adjective that describes the first image. Allow 1 minute.

5. *Use the other image as a noun.* Find a noun contained in the second image. Allow 1 minute.

6. *Create a simile.* Create a simile. Allow 1 minute.

7. *Explore the simile*. Explore how your simile is true. Allow 2 minutes.

8. *Apply the simile to your situation or topic*. Apply the simile to your situation. Allow 3 minutes.

9. *Debrief*. Debrief the activity.

VARIATIONS

- *Assembled*: Form pairs. One participant chooses the adjective and one participant chooses the noun.

- *Sunny like a Raging Monkey*. Choose three photos. Two images inspire adjectives, while one inspires a noun.

- *Simile Madness!* Using two images, continue to generate as many similes as possible – for example: *Sunny as a Monkey, Hot as an Animal,* and *Bright as a Primate*. Continue until there are no more ideas.

- *Reverse Monkey*. After completing *Sunny Monkey*, reverse the two cards, finding an adjective in the noun image and a noun in the adjective image. *Sunny Monkey* might become *Wild Light*.

- *Lightning Monkey*: Shuffle the entire deck. Deal the first image and use it to create an adjective. Deal the second image and use it to create a noun. Write down your simile. Continue this through the entire deck, until you have 26 similes. Which best describes your situation? Which best suggests a solution to your problem?

- *As-Is*: Choose a topic or situation (see *Table A*). Create a simile that completes the sentence, "My topic is X like a Y," or "My topic should be X like a Y." Examples: "Leadership should be Sunny like a Monkey," or "Creativity should be Wild as Light." Ask the participants to explain their simile.

PLAY SAMPLE

Here are similes generated from *Photograph 1 - Skyscraper,* and *Photograph 2 – Female Runners* to describe strong leadership:

- Participants generated the following adjectives from the Skyscraper image: ominous, foggy, tall, leaning, sharp, powerful, awesome
- Participants then generated the following nouns from the Female Runners image: girls, joggers, athletes, rain, cars, traffic, weather
- Participants then generated these similes: Ominous as the weather, awesome as an athlete, powerful as the rain.
- Participant 1 then said, "To their followers, leaders are often as unpredictable or ominous as the weather. Leaders should be less threatening."
- Participant 2 said, "Leaders should constantly train and develop their skills to be competitive."
- Participant 3 said, "Like rain, leaders need to make sure the crops are watered and the dust is washed away."

What other similes would you make?

DEBRIEF QUESTIONS

To get the most out of this Photo Jolt, ask these questions:

- *How easy or difficult was it to create similes? Why?*
- *Was it easier to create adjectives or nouns? Why?*
- *What techniques did you use?*
- *What ideas did you get from the similes?*
- *What is the value of similes?*
- *How will you apply these ideas to improve your situation or product?*
- *How can you use similes in your communications?*

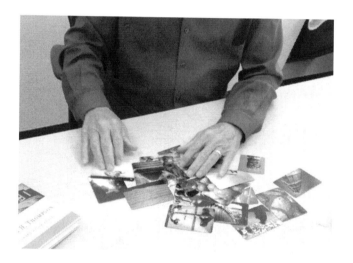

Looking for a simile

25

EYES WIDE OPEN

What questions arise when you approach a situation or topic with the eyes of a child?

Each of us suffers from the curse of knowledge in our areas of expertise. We overlook obvious aspects of our situation because we already 'know' the answers. Would we make different decisions if we looked at our topic with the eyes of a child?

SYNOPSIS

Participants pick a photo that is foreign to them and ask as many questions as they can about the image. They then do the same with their own situation.

PURPOSE

- ! *Clarity*: Ask powerful questions.
- ! *Creativity*: Generate as many questions as possible.
- ! *Conversation*: Discuss what it means to be open to ideas.

TRAINING TOPICS

- *Solo*: What questions do I have about this image?
- *One-on-One Coaching*: What questions do you have about this image?
- *Creativity*: What can I learn from this image or situation?
- *Observation Skills*: What about this image begs further exploration?
- *Psychology (Emotional Intelligence)*: What is it like to enter an environment with child's eyes?

PARTICIPANTS

- ✝ *Minimum*: 1
- ✝ *Maximum*: 30
- ✝ *Best*: 4 to 24
- ✝ *Configurations*: Solo, Pairs, Triads, or Groups

TIME

- ⏰ **< 5 minutes**: Run in pairs. Short debrief.
- ⏰ *5 to 15 minutes*: Run in teams. Full debrief.

PREPARATION

- Provide one deck of *Photo Jolts!* cards per 12 participants
- *ANYWHERE JOLT!* Run this Photo Jolt standing up, in a car, at a desk or table, or virtually.

VIRTUAL FACILITATION OPTIONS (SEE PAGE 21)

- ✓ Image Sharing without Cards
- ✓ Video Sharing with Cards
- ✓ Audio Sharing with Cards
- ✓ Remote Facilitation with Cards

FLOW

1. *Define the situation or topic.* Introduce the participants to the situation or topic of your meeting, workshop, or event (see *Table A* for possible topics).

2. *Choose photographs.* Choose an image that is foreign to you. Allow 1 to 2 minutes.

3. *Generate questions about the photograph.* Use the 'eyes of a child' to generate as many questions as possible about the image that you have selected. Allow 3 minutes.

4. *Generate questions about the situation.* Use this same mindset to ask questions about your situation or topic. What questions would a child ask? Allow 5 minutes.

5. *Debrief.* Debrief the activity.

VARIATIONS

- *Questions & Answers*: After generating your *Eyes Wide Open* questions, ask other participants to answer the questions that are raised.

- *Good Cop, Bad Cop*: Form Pairs. Raise questions about this image in the roles of 'Good Cop' (asking difficult, angry, interrogative questions) and 'Bad Cop' (asking easy, friendly, open questions). What's different about the two questioning methods?

PLAY SAMPLE

Here are five questions about *Photograph 2 – Female Runners.*

- *Why are they running in the rain?*
- *Why don't they have raingear?*
- *Why don't they take a cab?*
- *Did the rain surprise them?*
- *Do they like the rain?*

What other questions would you ask?

DEBRIEF QUESTIONS

To get the most out of this Photo Jolt, ask these questions:

- *How easy or difficult was this?*
- *Were any of your questions stupid?*
- *Do stupid questions have value?*
- *What are the stupid questions about your situation, topic, or product?*

26

BOOK BY ITS COVER

Can you judge a book by its cover?

They say you can't judge a book by its cover, but we do it all the time. How can we make the best of this instinct?

SYNOPSIS

Participants select a photograph. This photograph is the cover of a book your friend gave you. What is the title of the book? What is it about? Will you like it?

PURPOSE

- ! *Clarity*: Observe how natural it is for us to judge a book by its cover.
- ! *Creativity*: Generate book titles that match random images.
- ! *Conversation*: Discuss the pros and cons of judging a book by its cover.

TRAINING TOPICS

- *Solo*: Can I judge a book by its cover?
- *One-on-One Coaching*: Can you judge a book by its cover?
- *Communication*: What do images communicate about content? What drives us to judge a book by its cover? Are we good at it?
- *Creativity*: What could an image mean?
- *Design*: Surface or substance? Context or content? How can you leverage visuals to support the non-visual?
- *Sales and Marketing:* How do my visuals undermine my value proposition?

PARTICIPANTS

- *Minimum*: 1
- *Maximum*: any number
- *Best*: 4 to 32
- *Configurations*: Solo, or Pairs, Triads, or Groups

TIME

- *< 5 minutes*: Use as a quick icebreaker activity.
- *5 to 15 minutes*: Run in pairs. Short debrief.
- *15 to 30 minutes*: Run as a table activity. Full debrief.

PREPARATION

- Provide one deck of *Photo Jolts!* cards per 12 participants.

- Provide one *By its Cover Worksheet* per participant.

- *ANYWHERE JOLT!* Run this Photo Jolt standing up, in a car, at a desk or table, or virtually.

VIRTUAL FACILITATION OPTIONS (SEE PAGE 21)

✓ Image Sharing without Cards

✓ Video Sharing with Cards

✓ Audio Sharing with Cards

✓ Remote Facilitation with Cards

FLOW

1. *Define the situation or topic.* Introduce the participants to the situation or topic of your meeting, workshop, or event (see *Table A* for possible topics).

2. *Distribute photographs.* Give participants a random image. Allow 1 to 2 minutes.

3. *Set the scenario.* This photo is the cover of a book your friend just gave you.

4. *Determine the title.* What is the title of this book? Allow 1 minute.

5. *Determine the subject.* What is this book about? Allow 1 minute.

6. *Judge this book*: Will you like this book? Why? Allow 1 minute.

7. *Determine the reason.* Why did your friend give this to you? Allow 1 minute.

8. *What's your cover?* Choose a photo to be the cover image for your situation, topic, or product. Allow 2 to 3 minutes.

9. *Judge your situation.* How could others judge your situation based on the cover? How do you want them to judge it? Allow 2 minutes.

10. *Debrief.* Debrief the activity

VARIATIONS

- *Compact Disc by its Cover:* This photo is the cover of a compact disc that your friend gave you. What is the title of the compact disc? What band or artist recorded it? Will you like it?

- *Company by Location:* This photo represents the headquarters of a company. What is the company? Where is the headquarters? What brand message is the company sending? Is it an appropriate message?

- *Food by its Package:* This photo is the cover of a food package. Is it a boxed, canned, or bottled food? What is it called? Will you like it?

- *Movie by its Poster:* This photo is the poster for a movie your friend wants to see. What's the title? What genre of movie is it? Will you like it?

- *Tourist Brochure Cover:* This photo is the cover of a resort destination. What is the destination? Where is it? Will you like it?

- *Miracle Cure:* This photo is a picture of a miracle cure. What exactly is the cure? What is the disease? Will the cure work? How does it work?

PLAY SAMPLE

Here is an example using *Photograph 1 – Skyscraper* in a leadership workshop.

- *Book Title*: *Climbing to the Top*
- *Subject*: How to Climb to the Top of the Leadership Tower.
- *Judgment*: "I wouldn't like it. I don't think hierarchy is the measure of a true leader."
- *Why Did Your Friend Give You This?* "She thinks leadership is about hierarchy and keeps asking me when I'll be promoted."
- *My Situation*: "I must declare - to myself and others - that I can lead regardless of my position, title, or pay."

What other book ideas can you imagine?

DEBRIEF QUESTIONS

To get the most out of this Photo Jolt, ask these questions:

- *What is the relationship between context and content?*
- *What is the relationship between style and substance?*
- *Why do we judge a book by its cover?*
- *What are the pros and cons of that approach?*
- *What cover is your product, service, or company presenting?*
- *How might others interpret your cover?*
- *How do you want others to interpret your cover?*
- *Are you presenting your best cover?*
- *Should you change your cover?*

RESOURCES

- ☛ ***By its Cover Worksheet***: Download *Photo Jolts!* worksheets from *http://PhotoJolts.com*

BY ITS COVER WORKSHEET

What's <u>the Title or Name</u> of this?

What <u>Subject, Genre, or Type</u> is this?

Will I <u>like</u> it?

<u>Why</u> did someone give this to me?

If I could pick a cover, <u>which cover would I choose</u>?

What would I <u>name this product?</u>

27

BIZARRO WORLD

Can the worst aspects become the best?

We love rules that start with 'always' or 'never'; even though we know there are always exceptions. (Yes, there are even exceptions to exceptions). What is the relationship between our worst aspects and our best?

SYNOPSIS

Participants select a photograph that represents the worst of their situation or topic. They then turn that metaphor upside-down and use it to represent the best of their situation or topic.

PURPOSE

! *Clarity*: Demonstrate that good and bad are matters of perspective.

! *Creativity*: Generate alternative interpretations of a situation.

! *Conversation*: Discuss the fine line that exists between opposites like good vs. bad or genius vs. insanity.

TRAINING TOPICS

- *Solo*: Can I turn bad into good?
- *One-on-One Coaching*: Can you turn bad into good?
- *Philosophy*: Can I shift my perspective to see the good in this image?
- *Psychology*: Can I see the good in bad situations?
- *Sales and Marketing*: What opportunities are there in this seemingly bad situation?

PARTICIPANTS

- *Minimum*: 1
- *Maximum*: any number
- *Best*: 4 to 32
- *Configurations*: Solo, Pairs, Triads, or Groups

TIME

- *< 5 minutes*: Run in pairs. Short debrief.
- *5 to 15 minutes*: Run in teams. Full debrief.
- *15 to 30 minutes*: Run multiple rounds. Deep debrief.

PREPARATION

- Provide one deck of *Photo Jolts!* cards per 12 participants.

- *ANYWHERE JOLT!* Run this Photo Jolt standing up, in a car, at a desk or table, or virtually.

VIRTUAL FACILITATION OPTIONS (SEE PAGE 21)

- ✓ Image Sharing without Cards:
- ✓ Video Sharing with Cards:
- ✓ Audio Sharing with Cards:
- ✓ Remote Facilitation with Cards:

FLOW

1. *Define the situation or topic.* Introduce the participants to the situation or topic of your meeting, workshop, or event (see *Table A* for possible topics).

2. *Choose photographs.* Silently choose an image that represents the worst of the situation or topic. Allow 1 to 2 minutes.

3. *Return to seats.* After choosing images, participants should return to their seats to indicate they are finished.

4. *Share 'worst' metaphor.* Share the image and interpretation. Allow 1 minute per participant.

5. *Bizarro world.* This metaphor now represents the best aspects of the topic. Imagine how the metaphor is good. Allow 2 minutes. Note: participants should not create a new metaphor; they should reinterpret their existing metaphor.

6. *Share 'best' metaphor.* Share the image and new interpretation. Allow 1 minute per participant.

7. *Debrief.* Debrief the activity.

VARIATIONS

- *Cruel to be Kind*: Choose images that show how we can make our situation even worse ("We could move away from our customers, to this skyscraper in the city") and then use those images to become even better ("Then our customers would become more self-reliant").

- *Yin/Yang*: Select two images that show the best and worst of our situation or topic. Identify what our best and worst have in common. For example, the quest for artificial beauty can make us ugly, while embracing our ugliness can make us beautiful. Ask: Can one extreme exist without the other?

PLAY SAMPLE

Here is a play sample for *Photograph 1 – Skyscraper* in a Leadership Workshop:

- *Worst*: "Leaders look down from their ivory towers with no idea what we're doing here in the real world. As a result they make terrible decisions."
- *Best*: "Leaders sit up in their towers; unencumbered by the urgent distractions and short-term tactics that we're stuck in. They can take the long view and make decisions that are good for us."

What other statements would you make?

DEBRIEF QUESTIONS

To get the most out of this Photo Jolt, ask these questions:

- *How easy or hard is it to see 'bad' as 'good'?*
- *How can (or should) we utilize a contradictory perspective?*
- *Is this a useful skill?*
- *What are our best 'bad' opportunities?*
- *What other opposites should we explore?*

28

PRESENT

Is it really the thought that counts?

If it's true that gifts don't matter and it's 'the thought' that counts, we could give our friends anything and they would appreciate it. Right?

SYNOPSIS

Participants select a random photograph that represents a present. They decide what the present is, who is receiving it, and what the event is.

PURPOSE

! *Clarity*: Consider the presents we give to others.

! *Creativity*: Generate unusual presents for people we care about.

! *Conversation*: Discuss what a good present is. Debate the axiom that it's the thought that counts.

TRAINING TOPICS

- *Solo*: What is the thought behind my presents?
- *One-on-One Coaching*: What is the thought behind your presents?
- *Business (Engagement and Recognition)*: How can I recognize my colleagues or employees in ways that engage them?
- *Customer Service / Relationships*: Do I know my partner or client well enough to give them a thoughtful gift?
- *Psychology*: Does explaining 'why' change our perception of a situation? Does it change our response? Should it?
- *Sales and Marketing*: What does my target audience really want?

PARTICIPANTS

- *Minimum*: 1
- *Maximum*: any number
- *Best*: 4 to 32
- *Configurations*: Solo, Pairs, Triads, or Groups

TIME

- *< 5 minutes*: Run in pairs. Short debrief.
- *5 to 15 minutes*: Run in teams. Full debrief.
- *15 to 30 minutes*: Run multiple rounds.

PREPARATION

- Provide one deck of Photo Jolts! cards per 12 participants.
- Provide one *Present Worksheet* per participant.

VIRTUAL FACILITATION OPTIONS (SEE PAGE 21)

- ✓ Video Sharing with Cards
- ✓ Audio Sharing with Cards
- ✓ Remote Facilitation with Cards

FLOW

1. *Distribute photographs.* Give each participant a random image.
2. *Set the scenario.* Tell the participant, "This is a present you are giving to someone."
3. *What is it?* Participants must define what this present is. Allow 1 minute.
4. *Who is it for?* Participants then define whom this present is for. Allow 1 minute.
5. *Why are you giving it?* Participants define the reason, occasion, or event for this present. Allow 1 minute.
6. *Will they like it?* Will your recipient will like this present. Why or why not? Allow 30 seconds.
7. *Share.* Share your present and plans with your teammates. Allow 2 minutes per participant.
8. *Debrief.* Debrief the activity.

VARIATIONS

- *New Feature*: This is a new feature you're adding to your product or service. Which customer are you giving it to? Will they like it? How can you make it meaningful to them?

- *Target Recipient*: Name your gift recipient in advance. Choose a random card. Can you position this gift in a way that the person will truly appreciate it?

- *White Elephant Photo*: Write the names of all participants on cards (or use business cards). Ask each participant to draw the name of someone in this room. Choose a photo gift for them. Give it to them and tell them why you're giving it to them. This is a great closing activity for a conference and an excellent team icebreaker.

- *Go Deep*: Think deeply about your present by brainstorming five 'whats', five 'whos', and five 'whys' for your present.

PLAY SAMPLE

Here is an example using *Photograph 1 - Skyscraper*.

- *What is it?* This is a three-night stay in a hotel.
- *Who is it for?* It's for my customer.

- *Why?* He's an important customer who has given us great suggestions for improving our product. I'd like to get his suggestions on our new product.
- *Will they like it?* Yes. His company doesn't allow much travel. He recently mentioned he'd love to visit California one day. I think he'll like this and we'll get a great benefit out of it.

Who would you give this present to?

DEBRIEF QUESTIONS

To get the most out of this Photo Jolt, ask these questions:

- *What worked?*
- *How did you connect a random present to a person?*
- *What's the best/worst present you've ever received? Why?*
- *What's the most impactful present you've ever received? Is it different from the best? Why?*
- *What's the best/worst present you've ever given? Why?*
- *What's the most impactful present you've ever given? Is it different from the best? Why?*
- *Are you looking for ways to gift those who are important to you? What would happen if you did?*
- *What is a present? What is a gift? Is there a difference to you?*

RESOURCES

- ☞ *Present Worksheet*: Download *Photo Jolts!* worksheets from *http://PhotoJolts.com*

PRESENT WORKSHEET

What is this present?

      1.

      2.

      3.

      4.

      5.

Who could I give it to?

      1.

      2.

      3.

      4.

      5.

Why would I give it to them?

      1.

      2.

      3.

      4.

      5.

29

POSTCARDS FROM...

What do images tell us without words?

Postcards send implicit and explicit messages. If you couldn't read the writing on the back, how would you interpret the card?

SYNOPSIS

Participants receive a postcard from someone that's important to them, but the message is blurred. They then interpret the postcard.

PURPOSE

! *Clarity*: Interpret meaning from visuals.

! *Creativity*: Imagine what someone is writing to you.

! *Conversation*: Discuss the power of images without words.

TRAINING TOPICS

- *Solo*: How do I interpret visuals?

- *One-on-One Coaching*: How do you interpret visuals?

- *Communication*: How can I communicate my message visually? How should I read a visual message?

- *Creativity*: How many stories can I create from this postcard?

- *Culture, Diversity, Perspective*: How do audiences interpret visuals?

- *Sales and Marketing*: How do audiences interpret my visuals?

- *Training*: How do participants summarize our training using visuals?

PARTICIPANTS

† *Minimum*: 1

† *Maximum*: any number

† *Best*: 4 to 32

† *Configurations*: Solo, Pairs, Triads, or Groups

TIME

◔ *< 5 minutes*: Run in pairs. Short debrief.

◔ *5 to 15 minutes*: Run in teams. Full debrief.

◔ *15 to 30 minutes*: Run multiple rounds.

PREPARATION

- Provide one deck of *Photo Jolts!* cards per 12 participants.
- *ANYWHERE JOLT!* Run this Photo Jolt standing up, in a car, at a desk or table, or virtually.

VIRTUAL FACILITATION OPTIONS (SEE PAGE 21)

- ✓ Image Sharing without Cards
- ✓ Video Sharing with Cards
- ✓ Audio Sharing with Cards
- ✓ Remote Facilitation with Cards

FLOW

1. *Define the situation or topic.* Introduce the participants to the situation or topic of your meeting, workshop, or event (see *Table A* for possible topics).
2. *Select a 'Sender'.* Participants choose a person who can offer value to this topic: a customer, competitor, manager, teacher, father, mother, brother, or an expert. Allow 1 minute.
3. *Distribute photographs.* Give each participant one random photo. This is a postcard that they have just received from their sender.
4. *Interpret photograph.* Unfortunately, the back of this postcard is unreadable. Participants must interpret what this person is telling them about their situation or topic. Allow 5 minutes.
5. *Share.* Share conclusions with the other participants. Allow 2 minutes per participant.
6. *Debrief.* Debrief the activity.

VARIATIONS

- *Which Would They Send?* Choose an important person, like your biggest customer. Given your current situation and relationship, choose the postcard that you think they would send you today. Why would they send it? Choose the postcard you would send to them. Why would you send it?

- *Holiday*: This photo is a postcard for a real or imagined holiday. What is the holiday? Who sent it to you? What does it say?

- *For Your Eyes Only*: Choose a postcard you would send to someone in this room. Give it to them with no explanation. Have them interpret the card and let them know how close their interpretation is.

- *Postcard to a Friend*: Pick an image that represents your biggest learning from this event. Write the message that you'd put on the back. Example, "John, I'm in customer service training. Wish you were here. I learned that…"

PLAY SAMPLE

Here are three statements for *Photograph 1 - Skyscraper*.

The topic is customer satisfaction and the postcard is coming from my biggest customer:

- *Participant 1*: Our relationship isn't stable.
- *Participant 2*: The customer feels alone.
- *Participant 3*: The customer thinks we are distant.

What else would you say about this postcard?

DEBRIEF QUESTIONS

To get the most out of this Photo Jolt, ask these questions:

- *How easy or difficult was it to interpret your photo?*
- *What insights did you gain?*
- *How were your interpretations similar or different?*

RESOURCES

☞ **Thiagi.com**: Enter *'postcard to a friend'* in the search box
at *Thaigi.com* to find a written version of this game. Additionally,
Thiagi's 100 Favorite Games contains the 'non-photo' version, along
with 99 more games.

Performance specialist Emily Blunt shares her Photo Jolt at ISPI
http://YouTube.com/SMARTasHellVideo

30
CAPTIONS

Can you write a caption for this picture?

Captions placed under photographs attract people's attention and focus on the important elements. Captions take us from information to meaning. This game rewards players who have a talent for writing captions that are aligned with the theme.

SYNOPSIS

Players independently write a caption to go with a randomly selected photograph. A non-playing judge selects the best caption.

PURPOSE

! *Clarity*: Bring meaning to an image by adding a caption.

! *Creativity*: Create new meaning through captions.

! *Conversation*: Debate the attributes of a great caption.

TRAINING TOPICS

- *Solo*: How can I bring meaning (or new meaning) to this image?

- *One-on-One Coaching*: How can you bring meaning to this image?

- *Communication*: What's the best way to communicate this image?

- *Creativity*: How many captions can we create for this image?

- *Design*: How do I balance text with visuals?

- *Sales and Marketing*: What caption 'sells' this image?

PARTICIPANTS

- *Minimum*: 1

- *Maximum*: Any number.

- *Best*: 4 to 8

- *Configurations*: Solo, Pairs, Triads, or Groups

TIME

- *< 5 minutes*: Run as a 'write and share' icebreaker. No debrief.

- *5 to 15 minutes*: Run as a 'write and share'. Debrief.

- *15 to 30 minutes*: Run multiple rounds.

PREPARATION

- Provide one deck of *Photo Jolts!* cards for up to 250 participants.

- Provide index cards or sticky notes

- Provide paper and pencil

VIRTUAL FACILITATION OPTIONS (SEE PAGE 21)

✓ Image Sharing without Cards
✓ Remote Facilitation with Cards

FLOW

1. *Appoint a Timekeeper-Judge (TKJ)*. Select one of the participants at each table to take on the role of the timekeeper-judge (TKJ). Reassure the other participants that everyone takes a turn being the TKJ during the subsequent rounds.

2. *Display a card*. The TKJ selects a random card and places it in the middle of the table, photo side up.

3. *Write captions*. Players write a meaningful and memorable caption for the photograph within the next 60 seconds. The TKJ tracks the time and asks the players to stop at the end of 60 seconds.

4. *Rotate cards*. Participants hand their index cards to the person to their right. This stops participants from writing and encourages everyone to focus on the next step.

5. *Select the best caption*. Players take turns reading the captions they are holding. After the players have done so, the TKJ selects the best caption and gives its author the photo card. Remind everyone that the judge's decision is final and she does not have to explain her selection criteria. Alternatively, the judge can ask players to – on the count of three – point to the player with the best caption.

6. *Continue the game*. The next player assumes the role of the TKJ and repeats Steps 2 through 5. Continue the game until every player has been the TKJ.

7. *Debrief*. Debrief the activity.

VARIATIONS

- *Adlib*: Form teams of three to five participants. Select an image. Participants improvise a caption without duplicating previous statements. Continue around the group until they run out of ideas. Recognize the funniest, smartest, or oddest caption.

- *Caption Search:* Form teams of four. Each team writes captions for a random image. Exchange captions with another team. Each team searches the Photo Jolts! deck for the image that inspired those captions.

- *Duo*: Select two random cards. Participants create a caption for this pair of photographs.

- *Non Sequitur*: After brainstorming the captions for one image, apply those captions to a different image. Discuss the results.

- *Quotes*: Collect a series of famous quotes. Choose one and ask the teams to find an image that illustrates the quote.

- *Poster*: Once your group determines the best caption for an image, the teams design a graphic that combines the image and text. Who can create the best poster, coffee mug, or tee shirt?

- *Social Media*: Limit your caption to 140 characters.

- *Triptych*: Select three random cards. Participants create a caption for the trio of photographs.

- *Targeted Caption*: The caption must relate to the current topic.

PLAY SAMPLE

Here is an example using *Photograph 1 - Skyscraper.*

- *Participant 1 writes,* "It's a long way to the top."
- *Participant 2 writes,* "The leaning tower of metal."
- *Participant 3 writes,* "Technology overwhelms us."
- *Participant 4 writes,* "The bigger, the better."
- *Participant 5 writes,* "Living in the shadows."
- *Participant 6 writes,* "Who are the unlucky ones working at night?"

If you were the TKJ, which caption would you have selected?

DEBRIEF QUESTIONS

To get the most out of this Photo Jolt, ask these questions:

- *What types of images are easy to write captions for?*
- *What types of images are difficult to write captions for?*
- *How do different captions change the meaning of an image?*
- *How do different captions change the way you present an image?*
- *Which types of captions work best? Worst?*
- *How important are captions in your work?*
- *How do we see captions used in presentations and communications?*

RESOURCES

- *Thiagi.com*: Enter 'captions' in the search box at *Thiagi.com* to find this (and many other training games).

31
QUARTERS

Can you fill in the open spots with images that create a strong 'whole'?

It's easier to design when we can build an object from scratch. Are you able to build a strong design when two of the elements are pre-determined?

SYNOPSIS

Given two random photos and two open spots, the participants compete to choose two photos that create the best four-photo 'whole'.

PURPOSE

- ! *Clarity*: Think holistically while completing an existing project.

- ! *Creativity*: Design a working visual system using individual images.

- ! *Conversation*: Debate the meaning communicated by a visual system.

TRAINING TOPICS

- *Solo*: How can I create a 'whole' from these parts?

- *One-on-One Coaching*: Can you improve an existing system with new parts?

- *Creativity*: What's the most creative solution to this challenge?

- *Design*: What's the best design I can make given these limitations?

- *Customer Service*: How can I ensure a winning customer experience within my constraints?

- *Problem Solving, Decision-making, Critical Thinking*: Which parts best fit my existing system?

PARTICIPANTS

- *Minimum*: 1
- *Maximum*: any number
- *Best*: 3 to 30
- *Configurations*: Solo, Pairs, Triads, or Groups

TIME

- < *5 minutes*: Run as a solo activity with reflection.
- *5 to 15 minutes*: Run in pairs. Short debrief.
- *15 to 30 minutes*: Run as a table activity. Full debrief.

PREPARATION

- Provide one deck of *Photo Jolts!* cards per 12 participants.
- Provide one *Quarters Worksheet* per participant.
- Ask participants to clear table space for this Photo Jolt.

VIRTUAL FACILITATION OPTIONS (SEE PAGE 21)

- ✓ Image Sharing without Cards
- ✓ Video Sharing with Cards
- ✓ Audio Sharing with Cards
- ✓ Remote Facilitation with Cards

FLOW

1. *Determine teams.* Form teams of three to five participants.
2. *Distribute photographs.* Provide each participant with two random photos. Set the photos in any two open spots on the *Quarters Worksheet.*
3. *Spread out the remaining photos.* Spread out the rest of the remaining photos on a table.
4. *Choose photographs.* Participants silently choose two photographs that complete the design of their four-photo system and return to their seats to indicate they are finished. Note the level of competition for images. You might choose to highlight this while debriefing the exercise. Allow 3 minutes.
5. *Share.* Player one will lay down their two cards and explain the theme for their four-card system. Allow 2 minutes per participant.
6. *Continue.* The rest of the players will share their themes.
7. *Vote.* Have the players vote to determine who designed the best four-card system.
8. *Debrief.* Debrief the activity.

VARIATIONS

- *Titles*: Participants give a title to their final design.

- *Forced Upgrade*: Instead of starting with two random cards and allowing participants to choose their final images, have participants choose the first two images and then deal random photos to complete the system. Participants must then make meaning out of the resulting design. How does it feel to have an upgrade forced on you?

- *Surprise*: Deal two images face down on the *Quarters Worksheet*. Turn one image over and then choose an image that complements the first image. Turn the other image over – surprise! – and then choose the final image that will complete the visual system.

- *Three + One*: Place three random images on the *Quarters Worksheet* and then choose the final image that best completes the system.

- *Winning Customer Service*: Lay down two random images. Do these images represent good customer service, bad customer service, or a mix? Choose two more images that complete a winning customer experience.

PLAY SAMPLE

Here is an example using *Photograph 1 - Skyscraper, Photograph 2 – Female Runners, Photograph 3 – Ribbons,* and *Photograph 6 – Nature Path.*

- The participant receives two images: the Skyscraper image and the Female Runners image.
- The participant says, "These two images are low in color, so I knew I wanted to complete my system with bright colors. There was a building and people, but little nature or fabrics."
- The participant continues, "I chose the Ribbons and the Nature Path to bring complementary colors and subject matter to the final design."
- The participant concludes, "I gave the title *From One to Many* to this design."

What images would you choose to complete the quarters?

DEBRIEF QUESTIONS

To get the most out of this Photo Jolt, ask these questions:

- *How easy is it to upgrade an existing system?*
- *What makes it easier? What makes it harder?*
- *What strategies did you develop?*
- *Did you find any dead-ends? What did you do?*

RESOURCES

- ☛ *Quarters Worksheet*: Download *Photo Jolts!* worksheets from *http://PhotoJolts.com*

QUARTERS WORKSHEET

title

32

RISK ASSESSMENT

Have you considered all the risks involved in your decision or situation?

Experts conduct risk assessments, but often overlook the factors that later doom their projects. Why? Because experts know how things <u>should</u> happen when, in fact, many problems occur in blind spots. Are your risk assessments addressing your blind spots?

SYNOPSIS

Participants use random photos to brainstorm potential risks for a current project or situation.

PURPOSE

! *Clarity*: Identify risks to a current project or situation.

! *Creativity*: Brainstorm potential blind spots to consider.

! *Conversation*: Discuss potential risks to a project or situation.

TRAINING TOPICS

- *Solo*: What risks should I consider?

- *One-on-One Coaching*: What risks should you consider?

- *Business (Project Management)*: How can we mitigate our risks?

- *Creativity*: What could happen?

- *Leadership*: How can I spot the obstacles that might derail us?

- *Problem Solving, Decision-making, Critical Thinking*: What risks should we consider?

PARTICIPANTS

- *Minimum*: 1

- *Maximum*: 32

- *Best*: 4 to 12

- *Configurations*: Solo, Pairs, Triads, or Groups

TIME

- *< 5 minutes*: Run in pairs. Short debrief.

- *5 to 15 minutes*: Run in teams. Short debrief.

- *15 to 30 minutes*: Run the full activity.

- *30 to 60 minutes*: Run multiple rounds.

PREPARATION

- Provide one deck of *Photo Jolts!* cards per 12 participants.

- Provide flip charts and markers to capture actionable ideas.

- Invite appropriate attendees. Brainstorming requires diversity of thought. While this exercise encourages anyone to have creative ideas, it helps to invite a diverse set of participants.

VIRTUAL FACILITATION OPTIONS (SEE PAGE 21)

- ✓ Image Sharing without Cards
- ✓ Video Sharing with Cards
- ✓ Audio Sharing with Cards
- ✓ Remote Facilitation with Cards

FLOW

1. *Discuss current topic.* Set the context for the current situation that you are here to address.

2. *Create teams.* Form teams of four to six participants.

3. *Deal cards.* Randomly deal a photo card to each team.

4. *Describe.* Participants describe the image literally. Allow 2 minutes.

5. *Identify risks.* Participants identify the elements of this image that suggest risks. Allow 10 minutes

6. *Extend the metaphor.* Apply the identified risks – literally or metaphorically – to your current topic. Allow 10 minutes

7. *Debrief.* Debrief the activity.

VARIATIONS

- *Upside / Downside*: Identify risks and rewards for a project or situation.

- *Mitigation*: For each legitimate risk, use another *Photo Jolts!* image to brainstorm potential solutions.

- *Risk Sort*: Take all of your risks and sort them from 'least likely' to 'most likely'.

PLAY SAMPLE

Here is an example using *Photograph 1 - Skyscraper* for a discussion about reorganizing a company.

- *Participant 1 says*, "There is a risk of this skyscraper collapsing because it's too tall and unwieldy. Our organization might also collapse if it's too tall and unwieldy."

- *Participant 2 says*, "There is a risk of this skyscraper losing money because of a lack of occupancy. Our organization might also lose money because we cannot find enough talent to fill of our positions."

- *Participant 3 says*, "There is a risk of people jumping to their death from the skyscraper. Our organization has a risk of people quitting after the reorganization."

What other risks can you identify?

DEBRIEF QUESTIONS

To get the most out of this Photo Jolt, ask these questions:

- *What risks have we identified?*
- *How likely are these risks?*
- *What mitigation plans do we have?*
- *What mitigation plans do we lack?*
- *Do our mitigation plans have risks?*
- *How do we control the risks of our mitigation plans?*
- *What are our next steps?*

33

BUILD AN ORGANIZATION

If you built a new organization, what would it look like?

Most organizations are faceless. How would you build a strong visual brand for your own organization?

SYNOPSIS

Participants choose four cards: one for product or service, one for customer, one for workforce, and one for workplace. They then prepare and deliver an investment pitch.

PURPOSE

- !   *Clarity*: Define a visual brand for a company.
- !   *Creativity*: Create a pitch for a viable new company.
- !   *Conversation*: Discuss the importance of brand and brand focus in business.

TRAINING TOPICS

- •   *Solo*: Can I create a powerful brand and pitch?
- •   *One-on-One Coaching*: Can you create a powerful brand and pitch?
- •   *Business:* How do I visualize my new organization?
- •   *Communication*: How do I build a powerful verbal and visual message for a business?
- •   *Creativity*: Can we create a compelling new business?
- •   *Problem Solving, Decision-making, Critical Thinking*: What business can I build from these components? How will I pitch the business?

PARTICIPANTS

- †   *Minimum*: 1
- †   *Maximum*: Any number
- †   *Best*: 3 to 24
- †   *Configurations*: Solo, Pairs, Triads, or Groups

TIME

- ⏲   *< 5 minutes*: Run as a solo reflection activity.
- ⏲   *5 to 15 minutes*: Run in pairs. Debrief.
- ⏲   *15 to 30 minutes*: Run in teams. Full debrief.
- ⏲   *30 to 60 minutes*: Run with large groups. Deep debrief.

PREPARATION

- Provide one deck of *Photo Jolts!* cards per 6 participants.
- Provide one *Build a... Worksheet* per Participant.
- Ask the participants to clear table space.

VIRTUAL FACILITATION OPTIONS (SEE PAGE 21)

✓ Video Sharing with Cards
✓ Audio Sharing with Cards
✓ Remote Facilitation with Cards

FLOW

1. *Form teams*. Form teams of three to five participants.
2. *Set the stage*. Announce that the teams in this room will form new companies and compete for funding.
3. *Choose a product or service*. Each team silently chooses an image that represents their product or service and returns to their seats to indicate they are finished. Allow 2 minutes.
4. *Choose a client*. Participants silently choose an image that represents their customer or client and return to their seats to indicate they are finished. Allow 2 minutes.
5. *Choose a workforce*. Participants silently choose an image that represents their workforce and return to their seats to indicate they are finished. Allow 2 minutes.
6. *Choose a workplace*. Participants silently choose an image that represents their workplace and return to their seats to indicate they are finished. Allow 2 minutes.
7. *Create an investment pitch*. Teams now create a 1-minute investment pitch. Allow 10 minutes for preparation.
8. *Pitch your plan*. Allow 1 minute for each pitch.

9. *Debrief.* Debrief the activity.

VARIATIONS

- *Your Real Company*: Repeat this activity for your current organization. Is your organization as exciting as the one you just created? If not, why not?

- *Build Your Brand*: Choose three cards that represent your strength, the client you are sharing it with, and how you are sharing it.

- *Build a Sport*: Choose four cards representing the players, the field of play, the trophy, and one rule of a new sport.

- *Build a Country*: Choose four cards representing the flag, the president, the motto, and the natural resources of a new country.

- *Build a Religion*: Choose three cards representing the god, the church, one commandment, and one ritual of a new religion.

- *Animalize*: Give participants a photo of an animal. This is now their customer. How would they change the product or service for this customer?

- *Randomize*: Distribute random photos for each round and ask the participants to "Build a…" with the given resources.

- *Reinforce*: Reinforce DISC profiling, Tuckman's team model, and other models by debriefing the behaviors exhibited during the activity.

PLAY SAMPLE

Here is an example using *Photograph 1 - Skyscraper, Photograph 2 – Females Running, Photograph 5 – Umbrella,* and *Photograph 6 – Nature Path.*

- *Participant speaks*, "Hello ladies and gentlemen."
- *Participant shows Skyscraper*, "We're offering you a unique opportunity get in on the ground floor of a towering opportunity."
- *Participant shows Females Running*, "Our clients are trendy, active, and have disposal income. What are they missing?"
- *Participant shows Umbrella*, "Stylish umbrellas that make a statement while bringing color to their dreary lives."
- *Participant shows Nature Path*, "We have a community of village artisans who produce sustainable products for our customers and sustainable profits for our investors."
- *Participant concludes*, "Will you invest in us?"

What other statements would you make?

DEBRIEF QUESTIONS

To get the most out of this Photo Jolt, ask these questions:

- *What was easy or difficult about this exercise?*
- *How much did your business change as you gathered new images?*
- *How did you make decisions?*
- *Who led the team?*
- *What would you do differently?*
- *Which component of your organization do you feel best about?*
- *Which component of your organization do you feel worst about?*

RESOURCES

- *'Build a...' Worksheet*: Download *Photo Jolts!* worksheets from *http://PhotoJolts.com*

'BUILD AN ORGANIZATION' WORKSHEET

I'm building an Organization called:

Image 1: This is my product or service.

Image 2: This is my customer or client.

Image 3: This is my workforce.

Image 4: This is our workplace.

34

TIME MACHINE

Can you imagine this scene 100 years ago or 100 years from now?

Understanding how past actions brought us to our current situation enables us to understand how our current actions lead to future situations. Are you able to connect the present to the past and the future?

SYNOPSIS

Participants study a photograph. They describe the scene as it is today. They then describe what the scene might have looked like 10 to 100 years ago and what it might look like 10 to 100 years from now.

PURPOSE

!   *Clarity*: See how the current situation is an antecedent of the past situation and predecessor of the future situation.

!   *Creativity*: Imagine how a scene changes over time.

!   *Conversation*: Discuss our ability to understand the future or and past.

TRAINING TOPICS

- *Solo*: Can I see the past or future?
- *One-on-One Coaching*: Can you see the past or future?
- *Creativity*: Can I imagine the past or future?
- *Design*: How can I design for changing times?
- *Problem Solving, Decision-making, Critical Thinking*: How is my current problem rooted in the past? How will my current actions cause future problems?
- *Leadership*: How can I understand the past and predict the future?

PARTICIPANTS

- *Minimum*: 1
- *Maximum*: 30
- *Best*: 4 to 24
- *Configurations*: Solo, Pairs, Triads, or Groups

TIME

- *< 5 minutes*: Run in pairs or triads. No debrief
- *5 to 15 minutes*: Run in groups. Short debrief.
- *15 to 30 minutes*: Run in groups. Deep debrief.

PREPARATION

- Provide one deck of *Photo Jolts!* cards per 12 participants.
- Card selection works best for this activity when the *Photo Jolts!* images are spread out on an open table or surface.

VIRTUAL FACILITATION OPTIONS (SEE PAGE 21)

- ✓ Video Sharing with Cards
- ✓ Audio Sharing with Cards
- ✓ Remote Facilitation with Cards

FLOW

1. *Assign groups*. Form teams of four.
2. *Distribute photographs*. Shuffle the deck and give a card to each team. Ask each team to place the card in the center of their table.
3. *Visualize the past*. Imagine what this scene looked like 10 to 100 years ago. Allow 5 minutes for discussion.
4. *Make the connection*. Discuss what caused the scene to change or stay the same. Allow 5 minutes.
5. *Visualize the future*. Imagine what this scene looks like 10 to 100 years from now. Allow 5 minutes.
6. *Make the connection*. Discuss what causes the scene to change or stay the same. Allow 5 minutes.
7. *Share*. Share your past, present, and future states with other teams. Allow 2 minutes per team.
8. *Debrief*. Debrief the activity.

VARIATIONS

- *Alternate Timeline*: Change the past or future images. Determine what alternate timeline occurred?
- *Benjamin Button*: Distribute three photos. Define one as past, one as present, one as future. Explain how we moved from the past to the future. Reverse direction (past becomes future and future becomes past) and explain the transition again.
- *Time Warp*: Change the timelines in a way that suits your purpose.
- *Visualize*: Select the images that represent the future and past states of your present image.

PLAY SAMPLE

Here is an example using *Photograph 1 - Skyscraper*.

- *Participant 1 says*, "100 years ago, this was a rice field with farmers, oxen, and straw houses. It disappeared because of the industrial and information revolutions."

- *Participant 1 continues*, "100 years from now, this is a rice field again, farmed by part-time hobby farmers. The change occurs because technology and information combine to allow for a lighter industrial footprint that encourages citizens to reclaim land for personal use."

Do you have a different view of the past or future?

DEBRIEF QUESTIONS

To get the most out of this Photo Jolt, ask these questions:

- *How easy or difficult was it to imagine the past? Why?*
- *How easy or difficult was it to imagine the future? Why?*
- *How could we more easily make the connection from past to present to future?*
- *What is the value in making such a connection?*
- *What common themes were there in our conclusions? What differences did you see?*
- *What surprised you about the responses?*
- *How does this relate to your situation or topic?*
- *What was the past of your situation or topic?*
- *What is a potential future of your situation or topic?*

35

STAGES

How can we recognize the beginning, middle, or end of a lifecycle?

Everything – from trees to animals to companies to products – has a lifecycle. Everything has a beginning, middle, and end. How do we recognize and leverage these stages?

SYNOPSIS

Participants select an image and discuss whether it's at the beginning, middle, or end of its lifecycle. Later, they compare their findings with the current stage of their situation or topic.

PURPOSE

! *Clarity*: Recognize the stages of a lifecycle.

! *Creativity*: Imagine the lifecycle of an image. Apply metaphorical thinking to a current situation or topic.

! *Conversation*: Discuss the stages of a lifecycle.

TRAINING TOPICS

- *Solo*: Can I recognize whether this image is in the beginning, middle, or end of its lifecycle?

- *One-on-One Coaching*: Can you recognize whether this image is in the beginning, middle, or end of its lifecycle?

- *Creativity*: Can I visualize the other stages of this image?

- *Culture, Diversity, Perspective*: What do others see in this image?

- *Observation Skills*: What clues do I see in this image?

- *Problem Solving, Decision-making, Critical Thinking*: How can I best leverage the opportunities this stage offers? How can I make sure this image reaches the next stage?

PARTICIPANTS

- *Minimum*: 1
- *Maximum*: Any number
- *Best*: 3 to 24
- *Configurations*: Solo, Pairs, Triads, or Groups

TIME

- *< 5 minutes*: Run in pairs. No debrief.
- *5 to 15 minutes*: Run in triads. Short debrief.
- *15 to 30 minutes*: Run in teams. Full debrief.

PREPARATION

- Provide one deck of *Photo Jolts!* cards for 150 to 250 participants.
- Provide one *Stages Worksheet* per participant.
- Ask participants to clear table space for this Photo Jolt.

VIRTUAL FACILITATION OPTIONS (SEE PAGE 21)

✓ Image Sharing without Cards
✓ Video Sharing with Cards
✓ Audio Sharing with Cards
✓ Remote Facilitation with Cards

FLOW

1. *Define the situation or topic.* Introduce the participants to the situation or topic of your meeting, workshop, or event (see *Table A* for possible topics).

2. *Form teams.* Form teams of three to five participants.

3. *Distribute photographs.* Distribute a card to each team.

4. *Identify the lifecycle stage of the image.* Identify whether this image is at the beginning, middle, or end of its lifecycle and explain how you reached your conclusion. Allow 3 minutes.

5. *Visualize the other stages.* Visualize what the other two stages of this image look like. Take notes on the *Stages Worksheet*. Allow 3 minutes.

6. *Identify actions.* Identify the actions that would optimize the lifecycle of this image. Allow 3 minutes.

7. *Relate this image to current situation.* Relate your findings to the current situation or topic. Allow 3 minutes.

8. *Debrief.* Debrief the activity.

VARIATIONS

- *Three Images*: Deal a random image to each team. Each team identifies whether this image is at the beginning, middle, or end of its lifecycle. Teams then identify two additional images that represent the other two stages.

- *Three Stages of Life*: Distribute a random image to each team. Teams identify whether this image is at the beginning, middle, or end of its lifecycle. Distribute two additional random images that metaphorically represent the other two stages. Teams then identify what happened during this lifecycle.

PLAY SAMPLE

Here is a sample using *Photograph 1 - Skyscraper* for a mature organization:

- *Lifecycle stage*: "We believe that this image is in its middle stage."

- *Visualize other stages*: "The beginning stage would feature raw materials and construction workers. The end stage would show this building covered in graffiti and eventually being torn down."

- *Identify actions*: "We can prevent the premature end of this building. We need to create a strong neighborhood. We must maintain relevant clients. Finally, we need to keep the building looking new and fresh."

- *Relate this image to current situation*: "Our organization is also in the middle stage. It is neither young nor old. We must maintain relevant clients and keep our brand new and fresh."

What other statements would you make?

DEBRIEF QUESTIONS

To get the most out of this Photo Jolt, ask these questions:

- *What 'a-ha' moments did you have when thinking about the lifecycle of your topic?*
- *Have you thought about the lifecycle of your topic before this exercise?*
- *Are lifecycle changes typically easy or difficult?*
- *What can make them more or less difficult?*
- *How long will these stages last? Is that good or bad?*
- *Are you looking to speed up your transition to the next stage or to slow it down? What will trigger the shift?*
- *What strategies did you identify?*

RESOURCES

- *Stages Worksheet*: Download *Photo Jolts!* worksheets from *http://PhotoJolts.com*

STAGES WORKSHEET

What is the image of the BEGINNING stage?

What happened to create the transition to the middle stage?

What is the image of the MIDDLE stage?

What happened to create the transition to the end stage?

What is the image of the ENDING stage?

What needs to happen to extend (or quicken) the ending stage?

36
OPTIMIST & PESSIMIST

Can you see the positive and negative in a situation?

Optimists see the glass as half full. Pessimists see the glass as half empty. Which are you? Can you play each role?

SYNOPSIS

One participant finds the positive aspects of an image, while another participant finds the negative aspects.

PURPOSE

- ! *Clarity*: Discover the positive and negative viewpoints of a situation.
- ! *Creativity*: Imagine other viewpoints.
- ! *Conversation*: Discuss the power of perspective and interpretation.

TRAINING TOPICS

- *Solo*: Can I see positive and negative attributes of a situation?
- *One-on-One Coaching*: Can you see positive and negative attributes of a situation?
- *Business*: Can I view two sides of a potential deal or decision?
- *Creativity*: Can we brainstorm the positive and negative aspects of an image or situation?
- *Culture, Diversity, Perspective*: Can I see this situation from another viewpoint?
- *Philosophy*: How do we define bad or good?

PARTICIPANTS

- *Minimum*: 1
- *Maximum*: Any number
- *Best*: 2 to 30
- *Configurations*: Pairs, Triads or Groups

TIME

- *< 5 minutes*: Run in pairs with a 3-minute limit.
- *5 to 15 minutes*: Run in pairs. Short debrief.
- *15 to 30 minutes*: Run multiple rounds. Deeper debrief.

PREPARATION

- Provide one deck of *Photo Jolts!* cards per 24 participants.
- *ANYWHERE JOLT!* Run this Photo Jolt standing up, in a car, at a desk or table, or virtually.

VIRTUAL FACILITATION OPTIONS (SEE PAGE 21)

- ✓ Image Sharing without Cards
- ✓ Video Sharing with Cards
- ✓ Audio Sharing with Cards
- ✓ Remote Facilitation with Cards

FLOW

1. *Form pairs*. Form pairs.
2. *Choose roles*. One partner plays the optimist. One partner plays the pessimist.
3. *Distribute photographs*. Draw a random image.
4. *Optimist comments on image*. The optimist makes a positive statement about the image.
5. *Pessimist comments on image*. The pessimist makes a negative statement about the image.
6. *Optimist & Pessimist continue*. Continue making positive and negative statements until you run out of comments or the time period ends.
7. *Switch roles*. Select a new image, switch roles, and play another round.
8. *Debrief*. Debrief the activity.

VARIATIONS

- *26/26*: One participant is the optimist. One participant is the pessimist. The optimist deals an image card and says something positive about it. The pessimist then plays a different card and says something negative about it. Continue until you've played the entire deck.

- *Bi-polar*: An individual selects a random photo and then alternates between Optimist (making positive statements about the photo) and Pessimist (making negative statements about the photo). Which role is easier for you?

- *Duck Season / Rabbit Season*: Randomly switch roles in the middle of a round.

- *Optimist / Optimist, Pessimist / Pessimist*: In pairs, select an image. In Round 1, the two players say positive statements about the photo. In Round 2, the two players say negative statements about the photo.

- *Realist*: Play in teams of three. One participant is the optimist. One participant is the pessimist. One participant is the realist. Take turns addressing each image for your assigned perspective until three rounds have been completed. Deal a new image and continue.

PLAY SAMPLE

Here is an example using *Photograph 1 - Skyscraper*.

- *Optimist*: "This skyscraper provides many jobs in the area."
- *Pessimist*: "It blocks the sun from nearby buildings."
- *Optimist*: "That shade provides cooling shelter on a hot summer day."
- *Pessimist*: "The building uses too much power."
- *Optimist*: "The building also generates tourism in the neighborhood."
- *Pessimist*: "Which brings noise, pollution, traffic, high prices, and parking problems..."

What other positive or negative statements would you make?

DEBRIEF QUESTIONS

To get the most out of this Photo Jolt, ask these questions:

- *What was easy or difficult about this exercise?*
- *Which role was easier for you?*
- *Which role was more fun?*
- *How did it feel to have your partner continually fight you?*
- *People often say, "I'm not a pessimist; I'm a realist." Is there a difference? What is it?*
- *Does your current situation call for optimism or pessimism?*
- *What about your situation calls for optimism?*
- *What about your situation calls for pessimism?*

RESOURCES

- ☛ ***Photo Jolts! Video***: Watch Glenn and Thiagi demonstrate *Optimist & Pessimist* and see more *Photo Jolts!* videos at *http://YouTube.com/SMARTasHellVideo*

37

CLASSIFIED AD

Can you write a classified ad for an image?

The classified ad – used in newspapers or on the Internet – is an important sales tool that depends on the creation of a clear, compelling message. Can you create an effective classified ad?

SYNOPSIS

Participants write a classified ad for the items in their image. Later they try to sell their product to other participants.

PURPOSE

!   *Clarity*:   Write a short, accurate description of an item for sale.

!   *Creativity*: Create a compelling description of an item for sale.

!   *Conversation*: Debate the factors contributing to an effective sales message.

TRAINING TOPICS

- *Solo*: How would I write this classified ad?
- *One-on-One Coaching*: How would you write this classified ad?
- *Communication*: How do I communicate value to my target audience?
- *Language*: What words best sell a product?
- *Problem Solving, Decision-making, Critical Thinking*: What is the product I'm selling?
- *Psychology*: What bias do I have when creating an ad? Which product would I buy?
- *Sales and Marketing*: How can I sell this product?

PARTICIPANTS

- *Minimum*: 1
- *Maximum*: Any number
- *Best*: 4 to 28
- *Configurations*: Solo, Pairs, Triads, or Groups

TIME

- *< 5 minutes*: Run as a solo reflection.
- *5 to 15 minutes*: Run in teams. Short debrief
- *15 to 30 minutes*: Run as a full room. Full debrief.
- *30 to 60 minutes*: Run as a full room. Deep debrief.

PREPARATION

- Provide one deck of *Photo Jolts!* cards per 50 participants.
- Provide paper and pens
- Provide examples of classified ads from a newspaper or online

VIRTUAL FACILITATION OPTIONS (SEE PAGE 21)

- Image Sharing without Cards
- Video Sharing with Cards
- Audio Sharing with Cards
- Remote Facilitation with Cards

FLOW

1. *Choose photographs*. Participants silently choose an image that resonates with them. Allow 1 to 2 minutes.

2. *Return to seats*. After choosing images, participants should return to their seats to indicate they are finished. The facilitator may need to start a countdown – "One minute left" – to encourage participants to return to their seats.

3. *Set the stage*. Show participants images of classified ads from newspapers or the Internet.

4. *Write a classified ad*. Write a classified ad of 100 words or less for the product or service in their photo. Allow 10 minutes.

5. *Share ads*. Share the classified ads at your table. Allow 1 minute per participant.

6. *Select best ad*. Vote for the best classified ad at each table. Allow 3 minutes.

7. *Debrief*. Debrief the activity.

VARIATIONS

- *Blind Auction*: Write a classified ad for an image. Next, share your classified ads without showing the images. Ask other participants to bid for item, based on the ad. Which item would they buy? How much would they spend? After they see the image, are they happy? Did the ad work?

- *Random Image*: Instead of allowing participants to choose their own image, assign a random image.

- *Classified Competition*: Provide one image to each group of four. The four participants must silently write an ad for the common image. What were the differences in tone? What were the differences in product definition?

- *Reinforce*: Use this activity to reinforce Disc, Meyers-Briggs and other personal assessments.

PLAY SAMPLE

Here is an example using *Photograph 1 - Skyscraper*.

> ## For Sale:
>
> *Buy this 88-story building with excellent views and its own weather pattern! Impress your neighbors. Watch birds. Touch the clouds.*
>
> *Throw away your exercise machines. Heart-pounding activity is just one to eighty-eight staircases away.*
>
> *Give one floor to every friend or family member you have or selfishly rule your own towering domain. Remember, size matters!*
>
> *(Purchase now and we'll include 88 bottles of window cleaning solution and a parachute)*

How would you write this classified ad?

DEBRIEF QUESTIONS

To get the most out of this Photo Jolt, ask these questions:

- What are the strengths and weaknesses of your classified ad?
- What was difficult about writing your ad? What was easy?
- On a scale of 1 to 10, where 1 = completely accurate and 10 = completely inaccurate, how would you rate your ad?
- What makes for a great classified ad?
- How might you relate this experience to your product, organization, presentation, personal brand, or message?

38
KIPLING'S QUESTIONS

Can you answer six questions – what, why, when, how, where, and who – about an image?

Rudyard Kipling wrote, "I keep six honest serving men, they taught me all I knew, their names are what and why and when, and how and where and who." Can you use his servants to explain an image?

SYNOPSIS

Participants choose a random image and explain it by answering Kipling's six questions: what, why, when, how, where, and who.

PURPOSE

- ! *Clarity*: Accurately describe an image.
- ! *Creativity*: Imagine the image described by a narrator.
- ! *Conversation*: Discuss the importance of each of Kipling's six questions.

TRAINING TOPICS

- *Solo*: Can I report what's in an image?
- *One-on-One Coaching*: Can you report what's in an image?
- *Communication*: How might I best communicate an image?
- *Interviewing*: How can I best understand an image or situation that I can't see?
- *Leadership*: Am I asking the right questions?
- *Problem Solving, Decision-making, Critical Thinking*: Can I find this image based on the description?

PARTICIPANTS

- *Minimum*: 1
- *Maximum*: any number
- *Best*: 4 to 32
- *Configurations*: Solo, Pairs, Triads, or Groups

TIME

- *< 5 minutes*: Run as a solo reflection activity.
- *5 to 15 minutes*: Run in pairs or triads. Short debrief.
- *15 to 30 minutes*: Run in groups. Full debrief.
- *30 to 60 minutes*: Run two or more rounds.

PREPARATION

- Provide one deck of *Photo Jolts!* cards per 50 participants.
- Provide one *Kipling Worksheet* per participant
- Provide pencils or pens

VIRTUAL FACILITATION OPTIONS (SEE PAGE 21)

- Image Sharing without Cards
- Video Sharing with Cards
- Audio Sharing with Cards
- Remote Facilitation with Cards

FLOW

1. *Create Pairs*. Form pairs.
2. *Distribute photographs*. Hand each participant a random photo
3. *Choose roles*. Choose one partner to play the Kipling role and one to play the listener role.
4. *Close eyes*. Ask the listener to close their eyes.
5. *Describe 'What'*. In one sentence, Kipling describes what the image is. Allow 30 seconds.
6. *Describe 'Why'*. In one sentence, Kipling describes why the action in the image is taking place. Allow 30 seconds.
7. *Describe 'When'*. In one sentence, Kipling describes when the image takes place. Allow 30 seconds.
8. *Describe 'How'*. In one sentence, Kipling describes how the action in the image is occurring. Allow 30 seconds.
9. *Describe 'Where'*. In one sentence, Kipling describes where the image takes place. Allow 30 seconds.
10. *Describe 'Who'*. In one sentence, Kipling describes who is in the image. Allow 30 seconds.

11. *Return image*. Kipling returns the image to the deck and shuffles the deck.

12. *Find image*. The listener searches for the photo. Allow 1 minute.

13. *Summarize differences*. The listener explains to Kipling how the image is different than (or similar to) what they imagined. Allow 1 minute.

14. *Switch roles*. Kiplings become listeners. Listeners become Kipling.

15. *Debrief*. Debrief the activity.

VARIATIONS

- *Newspaper Columnist*: One participant at each table acts as a newspaper editor. Show one image to the group and ask the other participants to write a short article using the Kipling Worksheet. Which one will the editor choose?

- *Radio News*: Describe the image while your teammates search another *Photo Jolts!* deck for the image. Which teammate finds it first? To increase the difficulty, your opponent can forbid you from using 5 words of their choice in your description.

- *Kipling Interview*: Form triads. One participant is the 'witness', holding the image and answer questions. The second participant asks Kipling's six questions and guesses what the image is. The third partner acts as judge.

- *Combine with Police Artist*: One team member describes the image. The other three sketch the image. How do the three images differ?

PLAY SAMPLE

Here is an example using *Photograph 1 - Skyscraper*.

- *What*: "The image is a skyscraper."
- *Why*: "Lights are on because people are working late."
- *When*: "It's nighttime."
- *How*: "It's a misty night."
- *Where*: "It's a city."
- *Who*: "No one is visible."
- *Listener (after seeing the image)*: "I was surprised that the skyscraper was standing alone. I expected a skyline in a major city."

What other else would you say to describe the photo?

Could you find this image, based on the answers to *Kipling's Questions*?

DEBRIEF QUESTIONS

To get the most out of this Photo Jolt, ask these questions:

- *How easy or hard is it to describe the photo?*
- *What questions were most useful?*
- *What questions were least useful?*
- *How difficult is it - as a listener - to get an accurate image of the photo? Why?*
- *How difficult is it - as a communicator - to convey an accurate image of the photo? Why?*
- *What Kipling questions could you ask to better understand your situation or topic? Which Kipling questions would not be useful?*

RESOURCES

- ☛ *Kipling Worksheet*: Download *Photo Jolts!* worksheets from *http://PhotoJolts.com*

KIPLING WORKSHEET

What is this?

Why is it happening?

When is it happening?

How did it happen?

Where is it happening?

Who is it happening to (or with)?

39

SEQUENCING

Can you create order from chaos?

Much of life consists of organizing the disorganized, sorting the unsorted, and finishing the unfinished. Can you take random images and create a sequence?

SYNOPSIS

Participants take a group of random photos and sort them into their most logical order.

PURPOSE

! *Clarity*: Create order out of chaos.

! *Creativity*: Impose order where there is none.

! *Conversation*: Discuss what delineates order from chaos.

TRAINING TOPICS

- *Solo*: Can I create order out of chaos?

- *One-on-One Coaching*: Can you create order out of chaos?

- *Communication*: How will I create a story from random events?

- *Sales and Marketing*: How will I help others understand random events?

- *Training, Learning, Coaching*: Can I help learners make sense of the world?

PARTICIPANTS

- *Minimum*: 1
- *Maximum*: any number
- *Best*: 4 to 32
- *Configurations*: Solo, Pairs, Triads, or Groups

TIME

- *< 5 minutes*: Run as a solo activity. Short debrief

- *5 to 15 minutes*: Run in teams. Short debrief.

- *15 to 30 minutes*: Run in teams. Full debrief.

PREPARATION

- Provide one deck of *Photo Jolts!* cards per 5 participants.

- Ask participants to clear table space for this Photo Jolt.

VIRTUAL FACILITATION OPTIONS (SEE PAGE 21)

✓ Remote Facilitation with Cards

FLOW

1. *Create teams*. Form teams of three to five participants. Allow 2 minutes.
2. *Distribute photographs*. Deal 5 to 10 photos to each team.
3. *Create order*. Create a sequence with these photos. Prepare to explain your choices to another team. Allow 5 minutes.
4. *Share*. Share your thoughts and strategies with the other participants. Allow 6 minutes (3 minutes per team).
5. *Debrief*. Debrief the activity.

VARIATIONS

- *Chained*: Place the cards randomly on the table. Participants must make sense of the order without changing it.
- *Change the Numbers*: Use four photos, 10 photos, or 20 photos.
- *Story Remix*: Create a story from five photos and prepare to present to another team. When the teams gather, trade photo sequences. Each team now invents a story for the other team's photos. Discuss how the stories were similar or different. Debrief loss of ownership, desire to step in and interrupt, and the inability to listen to the new stories.
- *Storyteller*: One person comes to the front of the room and tells a story. The story could be a fable, a parable, or what they did last weekend. Teams must sequence five random images in a manner that best illustrates the story. Teams then present the visual stories.

PLAY SAMPLE

This sample uses *Photograph 1 - Skyscraper, Photograph 4 – Bloody Fish, Photograph 6 – Nature Path, Photograph 5 – Umbrella,* and *Photograph 2 – Females Running.*

- *Participant shows Skyscraper,* "One day two women left their office tower to go running in the countryside."
- *Participant shows Bloody Fish,* "They planned to get exercise and then eat fresh sushi."
- *Participant shows Nature Path,* "They didn't realize that the sun was so hot."
- *Participant shows Umbrella,* "They sat down under an umbrella and prayed for rain."
- *Participant shows Females Running,* "Soon, it started raining, so they ran back to the tower for their sushi lunch."

What story would you tell?

DEBRIEF QUESTIONS

To get the most out of this Photo Jolt, ask these questions:

- *What is order? What is chaos?*
- *How easy or difficult was it to make order out of chaos?*
- *Is this ability useful?*
- *Is there a danger in making order out of chaos?*
- *What methods did you use to create sequences? Did you use a time sequence? Did you use a narrative sequence? Did you use a cause and effect sequence? Did you use a problem and solution sequence?*
- *How did your team build the sequence? Were there disagreements? How did you resolve them?*
- *How would you sequence the story of your current situation or topic?*

40

AND THEN…

Can your team tell an interactive story based on random photos?

Few of us work in an independent environment. We often have to build on the work of others. Can you and your teammates build an interactive story using random photos?

SYNOPSIS

Participants collaborate to build a story, one sentence at a time. After a pre-determined number of sentences, a new photo triggers a change in direction for the story.

PURPOSE

- ! *Clarity*: Maintain a coherent plot line during chaos.

- ! *Creativity*: Improvise a story while adjusting to changes.

- ! *Conversation*: Listen and contribute to a collaborative work.

TRAINING TOPICS

- *Solo*: Can I master improvisational storytelling?

- *One-on-One Coaching*: Can you master improvisational storytelling?

- *Communication*: Can you improvise a clear story line?

- *Creativity*: How might you integrate diverse plot devices?

- *Teamwork*: How can the team build a better story?

PARTICIPANTS

- ♦ *Minimum*: 1

- ♦ *Maximum*: any number

- ♦ *Best*: 3 to 6

- ♦ *Configurations*: Solo, Pairs, Triads, or Groups

TIME

- ⏲ *< 5 minutes*: Run in pairs or triads for 3 minutes.

- ⏲ *5 to 15 minutes*: Run in groups. Short debrief.

- ⏲ *15 to 30 minutes*: Run multiple rounds. Full debrief

PREPARATION

- Provide one deck of *Photo Jolts!* cards per team.

- <Optional> Provide one die per team.

- *ANYWHERE JOLT!* Run this Photo Jolt standing up, in a car, at a desk or table, or virtually.

VIRTUAL FACILITATION OPTIONS (SEE PAGE 21)

- Image Sharing without Cards
- Remote Facilitation with Cards

FLOW

1. *Create teams*. Form teams of three to six participants.
2. *Roll die*. One participant rolls the die and notes the value.
3. *Select photograph*. Shuffle the deck and place the first image on the table.
4. *Start a story*. The first participant starts a story, delivering one sentence inspired by the photo. Start with "Once upon a time…"
5. *Continue the story*. Rotating clockwise, teammates continue the story for the number of sentences indicated on the die.
6. *Select next photograph*. After the team has delivered the number of sentences indicated on the die (one to six sentences), a new card is drawn. You can roll the die for a new number of sentences or continue with the number from the first roll.
7. *And then*. Continue building the story with new pictures. It helps to introduce each new photo by saying, "And then…"
8. *Conclude the story*. Finish the activity when every player has contributed three times, or when time runs out. Announce when the end of the exercise is approaching, so players bring the story to a satisfying conclusion.
9. *Debrief*. Debrief the activity.

VARIATIONS

- *Chain Gang*. Lay a deck of cards on the table. One player is declared judge. Player one plays a card and says one sentence. Player two has 15 seconds to play a card that continues the story.

The judge decides if the sentence is successful in continuing the story. Continue until a participant is stumped.

PLAY SAMPLE

This sample uses *Photograph 1 - Skyscraper*, *Photograph 2 - Female Runners*, and *Photograph 3 - Ribbons*, after rolling '2' with the die.

- *Participant one, photo one, sentence one*: "Once upon a time there was a tall, dark building."
- *Participant two, photo one, sentence two*: "The building was leaning and started to fall over."
- *Participant three, photo two, sentence one*: "And then people ran screaming from the falling tower."
- *Participant one, photo two, sentence two*: "So cars drove frantically through the pouring rain."
- *Participant two, photo three, sentence one*: "But when the tower hit the ground, it exploded into thousands of beautiful ribbons, like a rainbow."
- *Participant three, photo three*, **sentence three**: "No one knew that the building was a piñata."

What would you have said?

DEBRIEF QUESTIONS

To get the most out of this Photo Jolt, ask these questions:

- *How easy or difficult was this exercise?*
- *What did your teammates do that made it easier or more difficult to continue the story? Be specific.*
- *What worked? What didn't work?*
- *How did your approach change throughout the story?*
- *How important is the beginning of the story? The middle? The end?*
- *Did you get frustrated? Why?*
- *Did you find yourself giving up or giving in?*
- *What was the effect of giving up?*
- *What was the effect of giving in?*
- *How could you apply these lessons to your current work or life situation?*

RESOURCES

- **Photo Jolts! Video**: Watch Glenn and Thiagi demonstrate *And Then…* and see more *Photo Jolts!* videos at *http://YouTube.com/SMARTasHellVideo*

USE CASE

Improvising a Program Start

Facilitators know they must be ready for anything.

While in Chennai, India to facilitate a development workshop for 25 new college graduates, 'anything' happened to me. The session was scheduled to start at 9:30. With the room half-full at 9:29, I learned that the remaining participants were stuck in traffic and would not arrive for 15 to 20 minutes.

What should I do? I couldn't start the session without all of the participants and I didn't want the participants who were present to sit around bored, passive, and unproductive.

They knew each other, so a typical introduction exercise would not add value.

I pulled out my Photo Jolts! Deck and started playing "And Then..." at the right side of the room. We played for 15 minutes, working around the room and involving all of the attendees. The exercise introduced me to the attendees, created an energized atmosphere, and sent a clear signal that this workshop wasn't business as usual.

That's just one reason why I always carry a deck of Photo Jolts...

- Glenn

41

PROBLEM / SOLUTION

Given a problem, can you find a solution?

Much of work consists of complications we must overcome. Given a problem, where will you find a solution?

SYNOPSIS

Participants receive a random image. They identify problems, challenges, complications, and opportunities in the image. They then select an image that offers a resolution.

PURPOSE

! *Clarity*: Define a problem and solution set.

! *Creativity*: Generate as many solutions as possible.

! *Conversation*: Discuss different perspectives on problem solving.

TRAINING TOPICS

- *Solo*: How strong are my problem-spotting and problem-solving skills?

- *One-on-One Coaching*: How strong are your problem-spotting and problem-solving skills?

- *Creativity*: How many solutions can you find to this problem?

- *Observation Skills*: How many solutions exist in our environment?

- *Problem Solving, Decision-making, Critical Thinking*: What problems, challenges, opportunities, or complications does this image present?

PARTICIPANTS

- *Minimum*: 1
- *Maximum*: any number
- *Best*: 4 to 32
- *Configurations*: Solo, Pairs, Triads, or Groups

TIME

- *< 5 minutes*: Run using the standard flow.
- *5 to 15 minutes*: Run in groups. Full debrief.
- *15 to 30 minutes*: Run multiple rounds.

PREPARATION

- Provide one deck of *Photo Jolts!* cards for each 2 participants.

VIRTUAL FACILITATION OPTIONS (SEE PAGE 21)

- Image Sharing without Cards
- Remote Facilitation with Cards

FLOW

1. *Form Pairs*. Form pairs. Each pair gets a *Photo Jolts!* deck.
2. *Choose photographs*. Each pair selects one random image.
3. *Identify problems*. Each pair identifies problems, challenges, complications and opportunities in the image. Allow 1 minute.
4. *Identify solutions*. Find at least one image that addresses the problem. Allow 1 minute.
5. *Continue*. Continue to identify problems and solutions within the images. Select new images as necessary. Allow 5 minutes.
6. *Debrief*. Debrief the activity.

VARIATIONS

- *Complication*: In adventure films, the hero solves one complication after another until he or she reaches the final goal. As the hero, your partner gives you an image that presents a problem. You solve that problem with another image. Your partner then presents you with a new problem/image to solve. Continue until you cannot solve a problem. If you finish all 54 images, you win!
- *Combine with Risk Assessment:* Combine *Problem/Solution* with *Risk Assessment* for longer play and deeper discussion.

PLAY SAMPLE

This sample uses *Photograph 1 - Skyscraper* and *Photograph 2 – Female Runners*.

- *Participant 1 selects the Skyscraper and says*, "I see many problems here. The building is tilted and falling. There is smoke, so the building is burning. And many of the lights have gone out."
- *Participant 2 selects the Female Runners and says*, "I see many solutions to your problem here. People can run away. We can shower rain on the fire. We can wait for daylight in the morning. We can call a taxi and go home."

What other problems and solutions do you see?

DEBRIEF QUESTIONS

To get the most out of this Photo Jolt, ask these questions:

- *What about this exercise surprised you?*
- *How easy or difficult is it to find problems?*
- *How easy or difficult is it to find solutions?*

42

POLICE ARTIST

Can you describe an image well enough for someone else to sketch it?

Eyewitness accounts are important but unreliable. How difficult is it to describe a scene so that it is drawn accurately?

SYNOPSIS

Participants choose a random image and describe it to three artists. The artists draw the image and then compare their work to the original image.

PURPOSE

! *Clarity*: Accurately describe a sketch to an artist.

! *Creativity*: Imagine an image described by an eyewitness.

! *Conversation*: Discuss the difficulty of seeing what others describe.

TRAINING TOPICS

- *Solo*: Can I describe or sketch this image?
- *One-on-One Coaching*: Can you describe or sketch this image?
- *Business*: How do I get an employee, customer, or vendor to see the picture that's in my head?
- *Communication*: How can I communicate this image? How does feedback improve my results?
- *Interviewing*: Can I interview a witness to draw out what was happening in a scene?
- *Problem Solving, Decision-making, Critical Thinking*: Can I sketch this image based on the description?

PARTICIPANTS

⭫ *Minimum*: 2

⭫ *Maximum*: any number

⭫ *Best*: 4 to 32

⭫ *Configurations*: Pairs, Triads, or Groups

TIME

🕐 *< 5 minutes*: Run one round. No debrief.

🕐 *5 to 15 minutes*: Run four rounds. Short debrief.

🕐 *15 to 30 minutes*: Run four rounds. Full debrief.

PREPARATION

- Provide one deck of *Photo Jolts!* cards per 12 participants.
- Provide paper and pens or pencils for participants.
- Ask participants to clear table space for this Photo Jolt.

VIRTUAL FACILITATION OPTIONS (SEE PAGE 21)

- Remote Facilitation with Cards

FLOW

1. *Create teams*. Form teams of four.
2. *Distribute photographs*. Each team gets a *Photo Jolts!* deck.
3. *Choose the witness*. One participant on each team plays the witness. The other three members are police artists. Everyone gets to be a witness in subsequent rounds. The witness should not see the images being drawn and the artists should not see the card that the witness is holding.
4. *Choose a card*. The witness pulls a random photo from the deck.
5. *Describe the scene*. The witness describes the scene as the artists sketch. Artists are allowed to ask questions. Allow 3 minutes.
6. *Review results*. The artists share their images with each other and the witness. Allow the artists to see the original image.
7. *Summarize differences*. The artists tell the witness how the image differed from what they imagined.
8. *Switch roles*. The witness becomes an artist while one artist becomes the next witness.
9. *Play four rounds*. Allow each artist to play the witness.
10. *Debrief*. Debrief the activity.

VARIATIONS

- *Silent Sketch*: Artists cannot ask questions. Allow only one-way communication.
- *Feedback*: Allow the witness to watch the artists draw and provide the artists with feedback.
- *Reliable Witness?* Show each participant an image for one minute. Later, they describe their image to the *Police Artist*. How accurate is their memory after time passes?
- *Combine with Open & Closed Case:* Combine *Police Artist* with *Open & Closed Case* to reinforce interviewing skills.

PLAY SAMPLE

This samples uses *Photograph 1 - Skyscraper*.

- *The witness says*, "There is a tower. It's really tall. It's angled to the right. And it's nighttime. Some of the lights are on. Most of the lights are not. It looks a little foggy."

POLICE ARTIST | 283

How accurate do you expect the drawing to be?

What else would you say to describe the photo?

DEBRIEF QUESTIONS

To get the most out of this Photo Jolt, ask these questions:

- *How different were your drawings from the original? Why?*
- *How different were your drawings from each other? Why?*
- *How similar were your drawings to the original? Why?*
- *How similar were your drawings to each other? Why?*
- *What is easy or difficult about this?*
- *How effective is our memory?*
- *How much of success depends on the artist?*
- *How much of success depends on the witness?*
- *What's working or not working in the process?*
- *What is the effect of two-way conversation vs. one-way conversation?*
- *How is this challenge similar to the challenges in your environment?*

43
WHITE SPACE

What does each of us see 'outside the frame'?

We often make decisions based on a limited viewpoint. To do so, we must make assumptions about what lies outside of our field of view. What do you see outside the frame of a random image?

SYNOPSIS

Participants study a photograph and visualize what is outside the frame – above, below, to the left and to the right. Later they share their assumptions and visualizations.

PURPOSE

! *Clarity*: State assumptions we make based on what we know.

! *Creativity*: Imagine what is happening outside the frame.

! *Conversation*: Discuss what exists outside the frame.

TRAINING TOPICS

• *Solo*: What is outside my field-of-view?

• *One-on-One Coaching*: What is outside your field-of-view?

• *Icebreaker*: What questions would I like to have answered today?

• *Creativity*: What am I missing when I focus on what I can see?

• *Customer Service*: What might my customer see that I don't?

• *Leadership*: What opportunities or challenges lie outside my field-of-view?

• *Problem Solving, Decision-making, Critical Thinking*: What 'demons' lie outside my field-of-view?

PARTICIPANTS

✝ *Minimum*: 1

✝ *Maximum*: 28

✝ *Best*: 4 to 16

✝ *Configurations*: Solo, Pairs, Triads, or Groups

TIME

🕐 *< 5 minutes:* Single round. No debrief.

🕐 *5 to 15 minutes*: Single round. Short debrief.

🕐 *15 to 30 minutes*: Multiple rounds. Deep debrief.

PREPARATION

- Prepare one *Photo Jolts!* card per 4 participants.

- Provide one *White Space Worksheet* per team

- Ask participants to clear table space for this Photo Jolt.

- <Optional> Provide large sheets of white paper

- <Optional> Provide pens and markers

VIRTUAL FACILITATION OPTIONS (SEE PAGE 21)

✓ Image Sharing without Cards

✓ Remote Facilitation with Cards

FLOW

1. *Assign groups*. Form teams of four participants.

2. *Distribute photographs*. Shuffle the deck and give a card to each team. Each team should place the card in the center of their table (or in the center of the *White Space Worksheet*).

3. *Assign roles*. Each team member is responsible for 25% of the 'off-the-map' area. One participant is responsible for the area above the image. The second participant is responsible for the area below the image. The third is responsible for the area to the left of the image. The fourth is responsible for the area to the right of the image.

4. *Visualize what is outside the frame*. Visualize what is outside the frame and record your thoughts in the *White Space Worksheet*. Allow 5 to 10 minutes.

5. *<Optional> Draw*. Draw what you see outside the frame.

6. *Share*. Share what you see outside the frame with other participants. Allow 1 to 2 minutes per participant.

7. *Debrief*. Debrief the activity.

VARIATIONS

- *Demons Lie Here*: Ancient mapmakers couldn't see what was across the oceans and often assumed the worst. What is the worst-case scenario for what lies off your map? What fears are ridiculous? What fears are reasonable? Draw them.

- *Fill-in-the-Blanks*: As a session opener, participants choose an image that represents their current situation. Place it in the center of the frame. Generate four questions. Ask what happened in the past, what's going on now, what is in the near future, and what is in distant future? Or ask what is happening at the executive level, the front line, the customer site, and the peer level? Use these questions to drive the agenda of the session.

- *In Front of my Nose:* After completing *White Space*, remove the center image. Propose that we can spend so much time looking at our surroundings that we can miss what's right in front of us. Take a random photo and place it in the center of the whitespace map. Ask how this image fits in the center of this view. Are we looking through a microscope? A telescope? A periscope?

- *White Space Artist*: Cover the table with white paper. Place the photograph in the center of the white paper. Four participants draw what is outside the frame. Participants vote for 'most likely' and 'most creative'.

- *White Space Mash Up*: Project an image. Assign participants a number from 1 to 4 (1 = above, 2 = below, 3 = left, 4 = right) and ask them to draw their section of the white space. Mix and match the drawings from table to table to create new mash-ups.

PLAY SAMPLE

Here are four statements about *Photograph 1 - Skyscraper*.

- *Participant 1 says*, "Above this skyscraper, I see a full moon and the constellation of Orion."
- *Participant 2 says*, "To the right of this skyscraper, I see a children's park blocked from the sun by the tower."
- *Participant 3 says*, "Below this skyscraper, I see a community of homeless people and windshield washers who are begging from the workers in the building."
- *Participant 4 says*, "To the left of this skyscraper picture, I see a thriving theater district that offers arts to the community."

What other statements would you make?

DEBRIEFING

To get the most out of this Photo Jolt, ask these questions:

- *Did you all see the same things outside the frame?*
- *Which views surprised you?*
- *What caused your similar responses?*
- *What caused your different responses?*
- *What was your biggest discovery during this exercise?*
- *How does this thinking process fit into your work or life situation?*

RESOURCES

- ☞ **White Space Worksheet**: Download *Photo Jolts!* worksheets from *http://PhotoJolts.com*

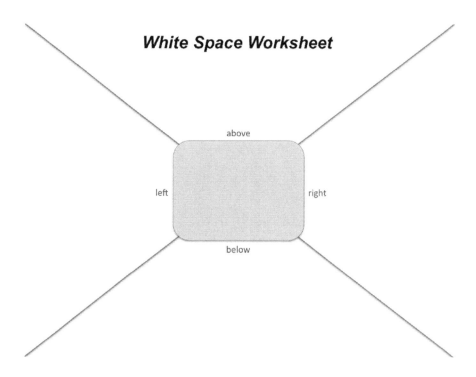

44

REDRAW

Can you communicate through drawing?

Words don't always work. When they fail us, we often resort to drawing on napkins, whiteboards, even in the dirt. When needed, can you solve a problem by drawing?

SYNOPSIS

Participants memorize a photo and then redraw it in 30 seconds. Their partner must then find the image within 30 seconds.

PURPOSE

! *Clarity*: Communicate with a partner using images.

! *Creativity*: Identify the essence of an image.

! *Conversation*: Discuss the power of abstraction.

TRAINING TOPICS

- *Solo*: Can I communicate through drawing?

- *One-on-One Coaching*: Can you communicate through drawing?

- *Art*: Am I an artist? What is an artist? What are our definitions of art, design, craft, and communication?

- *Communications*: How do I communicate without words?

- *Design:* What purpose do graphics serve? What graphics best serve my purpose?

- *Problem Solving, Decision-making, Critical Thinking*: What is the essence of this image? What is the minimum I must draw to communicate?

PARTICIPANTS

† *Minimum*: 2

† *Maximum*: any number

† *Best*: 4 to 32

† *Configurations*: Pairs, Triads, or Groups

TIME

◔ *Less than 5 minutes*: Single round. Short debrief.

◔ *5 to 15 minutes*: Multiple rounds. Full debrief.

PREPARATION

- Provide one deck of *Photo Jolts!* cards per participant.
- Provide paper, and pens or pencils.
- Ask participants to clear table space for this Photo Jolt.

VIRTUAL FACILITATION OPTIONS (SEE PAGE 21)

- ✓ Video Sharing with Cards
- ✓ Remote Facilitation with Cards

FLOW

1. *Distribute Photo Jolts! decks.* Give each participant a shuffled *Photo Jolts!* deck.

2. *Deal image.* Each participant takes one random photo.

3. *Set the timer.* Participants get 30 seconds for the next action.

4. *Memorize image.* Participants now study their photos. Allow 30 seconds.

5. *Return image.* Participants return their photos and shuffle the decks thoroughly.

6. *Set the timer.* Participants get 30 seconds for the next action.

7. *Draw image.* Participants draw their photos. Allow 30 seconds.

8. *Sign image.* Participants now sign their drawings.

9. *Collect images.* Collect the drawings and redistribute them randomly, face down.

10. *Set the timer.* Participants get 30 seconds for the next action.

11. *Identify images.* Participants turn over the drawings and search their deck for the matching photo.

12. *Validate.* Participants find the creator of the drawing to validate that they identified the correct photo. Allow 2 minutes.

13. *Debrief.* Debrief the activity.

VARIATIONS

- *Icons*: Extend this activity by creating icons – the simplest possible image – for the situation or topic.

- *One line at a time*: Form teams with three participants. Participants one and two select an image, view it for 30 seconds, and then put it back in the deck. They give the deck to participant three. The pair then draws the image with each partner contributing one line at a time. As they draw, the third player searches for the image.

- *Telephone*: Player one views a photo for 15 seconds and then returns it to the deck. Player one then has 15 seconds to draw a picture of the photo. Player one shows the drawing to player two for 15 seconds. Player two draws another image and shows it to player three for 15 seconds. Continue this pattern to the last player. The last player searches for the original image in the deck.

PLAY SAMPLE

This sample shows a drawing of *Photograph 2 – Females Running*.

Would you recognize the drawing?

DEBRIEF QUESTIONS

To get the most out of this Photo Jolt, ask these questions:

- *What were your thoughts during this activity?*
- *How many of you were successful? How many were surprised by your success or failure?*
- *What worked? What didn't work?*
- *What surprised you?*
- *What were your strategies?*
- *Are you an artist?*
- *Is drawing an important skill?*
- *Is artistic talent necessary to communicate visually?*
- *How tolerant is our brain of messy, abstract images?*
- *Are icons important?*
- *What are your icons?*

45

HALF-LIFE

How concise can you make your summary?

Brevity is difficult for many. Mark Twain for example, once wrote, "If I had more time, I would write a shorter letter." How will you edit your summary down to one image?

SYNOPSIS

Participants choose four to sixteen images that summarize a situation or topic. They then reduce the number of images in half, and in half again, until they reach a single image.

PURPOSE

! *Clarity*: Edit a lengthy summary to its essence.

! *Creativity*: Generate solutions under tightening constraints.

! *Conversation*: Discuss editing, brevity, and constraints.

TRAINING TOPICS

- *Solo*: Can I edit my thoughts?

- *One-on-One Coaching*: Can you edit your thoughts?

- *Communication*: How do I edit with an audience in mind?

- *Creativity*: Can I summarize content with one image? Can I choose the most powerful visual metaphor?

- *Design*: How can I say the most with the least?

- *Teamwork:* Can our team reach consensus on a topic?

- *Training*: How do I ask participants to summarize content?

PARTICIPANTS

† *Minimum*: 1

† *Maximum*: any number

† *Best*: 4 to 32

† *Configurations*: Solo, Pairs, Triads, or Groups

TIME

⏲ *5 to 15 minutes*: Start with four images..

⏲ *15 to 30 minutes*: Start with eight images. Share each round.

PREPARATION

- Provide one deck of *Photo Jolts!* cards per 8 players.

- Provide table space.

- Set out the *Photo Jolts!* cards in advance of the activity.

VIRTUAL FACILITATION OPTIONS (SEE PAGE 21)

✓ Video Sharing with Cards

✓ Audio Sharing with Cards

✓ Remote Facilitation with Cards

FLOW

1. *Form teams*. Form teams consisting of four participants.

2. *Define the situation or topic*. Introduce participants to the situation or topic of your meeting, workshop, or event (see *Table A* for possible topics).

3. *Choose photographs*. Teams choose eight photographs that summarize the situation or topic that was covered. NOTE: Use four to sixteen images as the starting point, depending on time, number of participants, and complexity of your situation or topic. Allow 5 minutes.

4. *Return to seats*. After choosing images, participants should return to their seats to indicate they are finished.

5. *Summary 1*. Teams share their eight-photo summary of the content. Allow 2 minutes per team.

6. *Half-life*. Edit summaries down to four images that capture the content. Allow 3 minutes.

7. *Summary 2*. Teams share their four-photo summary of the content. Allow 1 minute per team.

8. *Half-life*. Edit summaries down to two images that capture the content. Allow 2 minutes.

9. *Summary 3*. Teams share their two-photo summary of the content. Allow 30 seconds per team.

10. *Half-life*. Edit summaries down to one image that captures the content. Allow 1 minute.

11. *Summary 4.* Teams share their one-photo summary of the content. Allow 30 seconds per team.

12. *Half-life.* Teams should cut their photo in half... just kidding...

13. *Debrief.* Debrief the activity.

VARIATION

- *Surprise Audience*: What if your audience is executives? Would your image change? What if your audience is kindergarteners, bus drivers, Japanese students, or farmers?

PLAY SAMPLE

This sample uses *Photograph 1 - Skyscraper, Photograph 2 – Female Runners, Photograph 3 - Ribbons,* and *Photograph 4 – Bloody Fish.*

Round 1:

- Team shows Skyscraper, "Leadership means looking into the future."

- Team shows Female Runners, "Leadership means persevering."
- Team shows Ribbons, "Leadership means uniting diverse interests."
- Team shows Bloody Fish, "Bad leadership gets people killed."

Round 2:

- Team shows Bloody Fish, "Leadership is putting yourself at risk to reach a goal…"
- Team shows Female Runners, "…and persevering to succeed."

Round 3:

- Team shows Female Runners, "Leadership means exposing yourself to the elements while others play it safe."

What other statements would you make?

DEBRIEF QUESTIONS

If this activity is the capstone of an event, no debrief is required. Simply end with a round of applause and "Thank you. See you next time!" If you wish to debrief this Photo Jolt, ask these questions:

- What common themes did we see in our images?
- What paradoxes did we surface during our sharing?
- What surprised you in the responses?

RESOURCES

- **Thiagi.com**: Enter 'half life' in the search box at *Thaigi.com* to find an e-mail version of this game. Additionally, Thiagi's book *Design Your Own Games and Activities* (Thiagi.com) contains a third version of the game.

46

AN OPEN AND CLOSED CASE

How effectively can you ask open-ended and closed-ended questions?

Interviews are an important method of gathering information for decision-making, problem solving, and analysis. How well do you use open-ended and closed-ended questions to gather information?

SYNOPSIS

Participants practice open-ended and closed-ended questions to gather information from a scene.

PURPOSE

! *Clarity*: Practice asking effective questions.

! *Creativity*: Solve a problem through effective questioning.

! *Conversation*: Discuss effective questioning techniques.

TRAINING TOPICS

- *One-on-One Coaching*: How effectively do you ask questions?

- *Interviewing*: How do open-ended and closed-ended questions facilitate interviewing?

- *Leadership*: How do I ask better questions to get better answers?

- *Problem Solving, Decision-making, Critical Thinking*: How important is questioning to accurate data gathering? How do I plan my questioning strategy?

- *Sales and Marketing*: What questions should I ask my customers?

PARTICIPANTS

† *Minimum*: 2

† *Maximum*: Any number

† *Best*: 10 to 20

† *Configurations*: Solo, Pairs, Triads, or Groups

TIME

◷ *< 5 minutes*: Run *All Against One* Variation.

◷ *5 to 15 minutes*: Short debrief.

◷ *15 to 30 minutes*: Full debrief.

◷ *30 to 60 minutes*: Run multiple rounds. Deep debrief.

PREPARATION

- Provide one deck of *Photo Jolts!* cards per 5 pairs of participants.
- *ANYWHERE JOLT!* Run this Photo Jolt standing up, in a car, at a desk or table, or virtually.

VIRTUAL FACILITATION OPTIONS (SEE PAGE 21)

- ✓ Image Sharing without Cards
- ✓ Video Sharing with Cards
- ✓ Remote Facilitation with Cards

FLOW

1. *Distribute photographs.* Shuffle the deck and give three cards to each participant.
2. *Assign roles.* Form pairs. Player 1 plays the role of interviewer, while Player 2 plays the interviewee.
3. *Explain closed questions vs. open questions.* Explain that closed-ended questions allow the interviewee to say only 'yes' or 'no'; while open-ended questions encourage the interviewee to provide more depth in their responses. An example of a closed-ended question is, "Did you see a yellow car?" An example of an open-ended question is, "What did you see at the scene?"
4. *Play Round 1 – Closed questions.* The interviewer practices closed questions by asking the interviewee ten closed questions about the first photo. Continue until the interviewer gets ten 'yes' or 'no' responses. At the end, the interviewer guesses the subject of the photo. Allow 5 minutes.
5. *Play Round 2 – Open Questions.* The interviewer practices open-ended questions by asking the interviewee five open-ended questions about the second photo. Continue until the interviewer

gets five open responses. At the end, the interviewer guesses what the photo is. Allow 5 minutes.

6. *Play Round 3 – Mixed Questions*. The interviewer practices mixing closed and open-ended questions by asking the interviewee ten questions about the third photo. The interviewer should track their mix of questions for reference. At the end, the interviewer guesses the subject of the photo. Allow 5 minutes.

7. *Exchange Roles*. Have partners exchange roles – the interviewer becomes the interviewee, while the interviewee becomes the interviewer – and repeat the three rounds.

8. *Debrief*. Debrief the activity.

VARIATIONS

- *'H-O-R-S-E'*: Form teams of four. When a participant uses the wrong type of question, assign one letter of the word 'HORSE' to the participant. When a participant spells the word 'HORSE', he or she is ejected from the game. Continue until one player remains. Shorten the game by playing F-A-I-L or B-A-D.

- *Interrogation*: Form triads. Player one selects a photo. Players two and three compete to guess the photo first, by asking open and closed questions.

- *All Against One*: One participant holds the image. All other participants ask questions and guess the image. First player to guess the image wins.

PLAY SAMPLE

Here are four questions about *Photograph 2 – Female Runners*:

- • *Closed-ended*: "Are there animals in your photo?"
- • *Open-ended*: "What is in your photo?"
- • *Closed-ended*: "Are the trees green?"
- • *Open-ended*: "Why are the women running?"

How would you answer these questions?

What open-ended or closed-ended follow-up questions would you ask?

DEBRIEF QUESTIONS

To get the most out of this Photo Jolt, ask these questions:

- 🔎 *What advantages and disadvantages do closed-ended questions provide?*
- 🔎 *What advantages and disadvantages do open-ended questions provide?*
- 🔎 *What approaches worked for you?*

47

RECIPE FOR SUCCESS

What is your recipe for success?

Recipes allow us to plan for success. Can you create a recipe for your situation or topic?

SYNOPSIS

Participants select three to five cards that represent the ingredients that have made (or will make) them or their project successful.

PURPOSE

! *Clarity*: Describe the ingredients for your success.

! *Creativity*: Identify visual metaphors for the factors that allow you to succeed.

! *Conversation*: Discuss what is needed for success.

TRAINING TOPICS

- *Solo*: What is my recipe for success?
- *One-on-One Coaching*: What is your recipe for success?
- *Communication*: Can I share my recipe for success?
- *Creativity*: Can I turn my success into a recipe?
- *Leadership:* What am I asking of my followers?
- *Problem Solving, Decision-making, Critical Thinking*: What mix of ingredients is necessary for my program to work?
- *Training*: How can I create recipes for my learners?

PARTICIPANTS

- *Minimum*: 1
- *Maximum*: any number
- *Best*: 4 to 32
- *Configurations*: Solo, Pairs, Triads, or Groups

TIME

- *5 to 15 minutes*: Run as a solo activity. Short debrief.
- *15 to 30 minutes*: Run in pairs. Debrief.
- *30 to 60 minutes*: Run in triads or groups.

PREPARATION

- Provide one deck of *Photo Jolts!* cards per 3 participants.
- Provide one *Recipe Worksheet* per participant.
- Prepare to share a typical recipe from a cookbook.
- Ask the participants to clear table space for this Photo Jolt.

VIRTUAL FACILITATION OPTIONS (SEE PAGE 21)

- ✓ Video Sharing with Cards
- ✓ Audio Sharing with Cards
- ✓ Remote Facilitation with Cards

FLOW

1. *Define the situation or topic.* Introduce participants to the situation or topic of your meeting, workshop, or event (see *Table A* for possible topics).

2. *Set up the exercise.* Participants will write a *Recipe for Success'*. This recipe includes: one to three photographs representing the ingredients; one photograph representing the tools needed; one photograph representing the cooking method; and one photograph that representing the final meal. Remind participants to consider the amount of each ingredient, the serving size, and other useful information.

3. *Show a sample.* Show a sample recipe from a cookbook.

4. *Choose photographs.* Silently choose three to six photographs to include in their *Recipe for Success.* Allow 3 to 5 minutes.

5. *Return to seats.* Once participants have chosen their images, they should return to their seats to indicate they are finished.

6. *Write the recipe.* Participants now create their recipe and write it on the *Recipe Worksheet.* Allow 5 minutes.

7. *Share*. Share recipes with other participants.
8. *Debrief*. Debrief the activity.

VARIATIONS

-   *Mentoring*: A young employee approaches you and says, "I want to be like you. What is your recipe?" Create your recipe using three to six images.
-   *Retirement*: You are retiring. Before you leave, your company asks you to capture the recipe for success in your skill area (police work, singing, sales, engineering, teaching, etc.). Create your recipe using three to six images.

PLAY SAMPLE

This sample uses *Photograph 1 - Skyscraper, Photograph 2 – Female Runners, Photograph 3 - Ribbons, Photograph 4 – Bloody Fish, Photograph 5 - Umbrella,* and *Photograph 6 – Nature Path.* The topic is leadership.

-   One participant says, "This is our recipe for leadership."
-   *Ingredients*: "One half-pound of *Skyscraper* provides steely resolve and clear vision. One quart of partnership - like these *Female Runners* display - balances the harshness of the steel. Sprinkles of

color like those found in these *Ribbons*, because you can't lead in black and white. It leaves a boring taste."

- **Tools**: "Use a sieve – like this *Umbrella* – to remove distractions, negativity, and fear."
- **Method**: "Leadership is best served raw and authentic – like these *Fish*."
- **Meal**: "The final meal is a clear, well-paved *Path* leading to a sunny destination."

What other ingredients, tools, or methods would you consider?

DEBRIEF QUESTIONS

To get the most out of this Photo Jolt, ask these questions:

- *Are recipes useful? Why or why not?*
- *What makes for a great recipe?*
- *Is your recipe simple or complex?*
- *Is your recipe expensive or inexpensive?*
- *Is your recipe tasty or medicinal?*
- *How are our recipes similar or different?*
- *How long does it take to make?*
- *Which recipes do you like best?*
- *Could you follow these recipes and find success?*
- *How would you modify these recipes?*

RESOURCES

- **Review**: A cookbook for ideas on how to build a great recipe.
- **Recipe Worksheet**: Download *Photo Jolts!* worksheets from *http://PhotoJolts.com*

RECIPE WORKSHEET

Serving Size

Ingredients

Preparation

Directions

     1.

     2.

     3.

     4.

     5.

     6.

     7.

     8.

Tips

48

LESSONS FROM...

What can we learn from other disciplines?

Every discipline has its own tips, tricks, and traps. What would we learn if we transferred those best practices to a seemingly unrelated discipline?

SYNOPSIS

Participants choose a theme. They then choose a random image and create a one-day training with four topics inspired by that photo.

PURPOSE

! *Clarity*: Identify best practices for a discipline.

! *Creativity*: Transfer lessons from one discipline to another.

! *Conversation*: Discuss the power of transferring ideas across disciplines.

TRAINING TOPICS

* *Solo*: What might I learn from other disciplines?

* *One-on-One Coaching*: What might you learn from other disciplines?

* *Creativity:* Can I find a new way to convey a not-so-new message?

* *Design*: What can I apply from other fields to improve my design?

* *Problem Solving, Decision-making, Critical Thinking*: What might I learn from other disciplines?

* *Training*: How can we best teach, coach, or learn? How can we best reach our audiences?

PARTICIPANTS

✝ *Minimum*: 1

✝ *Maximum*: any number

✝ *Best*: 4 to 32

✝ *Configurations*: Solo, Pairs, Triads, or Groups

TIME

⏲ *< 5 minutes*: Run in pairs. Short debrief.

⏲ *5 to 15 minutes*: Run in triads or small groups. Short debrief.

⏲ *15 to 30 minutes*: Run as a full-room activity.

⏲ *30 to 60 minutes*: Run as a teach-back.

PREPARATION

- Provide one deck of *Photo Jolts!* cards per 12 participants.
- *ANYWHERE JOLT!* Run this Photo Jolt standing up, in a car, at a desk or table, or virtually.
- If this is a teach-back, provide table or wall space for the teams.

VIRTUAL FACILITATION OPTIONS (SEE PAGE 21)

✓ Image Sharing without Cards
✓ Video Sharing with Cards
✓ Audio Sharing with Cards
✓ Remote Facilitation with Cards

FLOW

1. *Define the situation or topic.* Introduce the participants to the situation or topic of your meeting, workshop, or event (see *Table A* for possible topics).
2. *Distribute photographs.* Deal each participant or team a random image, face down.
3. *Title your workshop.* Participants will create a 1-day workshop based on their situation and this image. They should title the workshop using the formula "X Lessons from *this photo.*" For example, "Relationships Lessons from a Skyscraper." Allow 2 minutes.
4. *Identify lessons.* Participants identify four lessons that this image teaches about their subject. Allow 10 minutes.
5. *Share.* Share workshop outlines with the other participants. Allow 3 minutes per team.
6. *Debrief.* Debrief the activity.

VARIATIONS

- *Conference*: Design a conference schedule, using four images to inspire the topics.

- *Presentation*: Design a presentation on your situation or topic, using 5 to 10 images.

PLAY SAMPLE

This sample uses *Photograph 2 – Female Runners* in a leadership workshop.

- *Our workshop title is* "Leadership Lessons from Runners."
- *Lesson 1 is* "A Little Rain Can't Stop a Leader."
- *Lesson 2 is* "While A Leader Leads, Others Stay Comfortable."
- *Lesson 3 is* "Always Have a Partner."
- *Lesson 4 is* "Leadership Doesn't Care About Age or Gender."

What other lessons would you suggest?

DEBRIEF QUESTIONS

To get the most out of this Photo Jolt, ask these questions:

- *Which of your lessons is the most useful? Why?*
- *Tell us how you would apply one of the lesson.*
- *Is there value in looking at other disciplines for lessons to apply to your discipline?*
- *Are there other disciplines you want to explore?*
- *Could you really create this workshop?*
- *Who could you target with this workshop?*
- *Would you attend this workshop?*
- *What else would you add to your workshop?*
- *Who should conduct the workshop?*

RESOURCES

- ☛ ***Lessons From... Worksheet***: Download *Photo Jolts!* worksheets from *http://PhotoJolts.com*

LESSONS FROM... WORKSHEET

Topic (e.g. Management, Love, Success):

Lesson Source (e.g. Joggers, Dead Fish, Umbrella):

Lesson 1:

Lesson 2:

Lesson 3:

Lesson 4:

49

TRAINING PHOTOS

How can you use images to explain the concepts from a workshop?

Many workshops use conceptual models or frameworks to teach. How can we explain these concepts with images?

SYNOPSIS

Participants choose images that represent the concepts in a workshop. They then share insights with other participants.

PURPOSE

- *Clarity*: Explain concepts through images.
- *Creativity*: Generate different perspectives on a conceptual model.
- *Conversation*: Stimulate group sharing and learning.

TRAINING TOPICS

- *Solo*: How well can I explain the concepts in this workshop?
- *One-on-One Coaching*: How well can you explain the concepts in this workshop?
- *Icebreaker*: How much do the students know about this subject?
- *Training*: What image best represents this concept? Did my students really learn this subject?

PARTICIPANTS

- *Minimum*: 1
- *Maximum*: any number
- *Best*: 4 to 32
- *Configurations*: Solo, Pairs, Triads, or Groups

TIME

- *5 to 15 minutes*: Run pairs or triads. Short debrief.
- *15 to 30 minutes*: Run in groups. Full debrief.
- *30 to 60 minutes*: Run as a teach-back activity.

PREPARATION

- The number of cards needed for this activity varies with the conceptual model. Typically, one deck of *Photo Jolts!* activity cards is needed per 4 participants.
- If this is a teach-back, provide table or wall space for the teams.

VIRTUAL FACILITATION OPTIONS (SEE PAGE 21)

- ✓ Video Sharing with Cards
- ✓ Audio Sharing with Cards
- ✓ Remote Facilitation with Cards

FLOW

1. *Set agenda*. Decide if this is an opening exercise used to discover how much participants already know; or a closing exercise used to review content that has been taught. For senior executives, this exercise could open a leadership course. For front-line employees or young leaders, use this as a review exercise after the participants have learned about leadership.

2. *Explain the model*. Teach the model that you are using in the workshop.

3. *Define teams*. Create one team for each piece of the conceptual model. SMART goals, for example, requires five teams. The SWOT model requires 4 teams.

4. *Choose photographs*. Participants silently choose a photograph that best represents their component of the conceptual model. Allow 1 to 2 minutes.

5. *Return to seats*. After choosing images, participants should return to their seats to indicate they are finished.

6. *Share images*. At each table, the teams share their images and explanations. Allow 5 minutes.

7. *Consolidate findings*. Table groups consolidate their findings and choose one image that best represents their interpretation of the conceptual model. Allow 3 minutes.

8. *Teach-back*. Table groups teach the concept to the other teams. Allow 2 minutes.

9. *Continue*. Each participant or team describes his or her concept through image and metaphor. Allow 2 minutes per team.

10. *Debrief*. Debrief the activity.

VARIATIONS

Modify this exercise to reinforce conceptual models. Here are a few that we've used:

- *SWOT Analysis*: Explain Strengths, Weaknesses, Opportunities, and Threats.

- *SCAMPER Brainstorming*: Explain the concepts of this brainstorming model – Substitute, Combine, Adapt, Modify, Put to another use, Eliminate, and Reverse.

- *Seven-Sentence-Stories*: Explain this storytelling model.

- *Organizational Values*: Explain your organization's values.

- *Leadership Challenge*: Explain Jim Kouzes and Barry Posner's *Five Practices of Exemplary Leadership* from *The Leadership Challenge*.

- *DISC Profiling*: Explain Dominance, Influence, Steadiness, and Compliance.

PLAY SAMPLE

This sample, from a SMART goal training, uses *Photograph 3 – Ribbons*, *Photograph 1 - Skyscraper*, *Photograph 4 – Bloody Fish*, *Photograph 5 – Umbrella*, and *Photograph 2 – Female Runners*.

- *Team 1 shows the Ribbons* and says, "This photo demonstrates *Specific*. If you want a ribbon, tell me which one."
- *Team 2 shows the Skyscraper* and says, "*Measurable* means knowing the start, the finish, and the distance in-between. This skyscraper has a bottom floor, a top floor, and you can count the floors in-between."
- *Team 3 shows the Bloody Fish* and says, "These fish were *Aggressively Attainable*. Someone spent a long day on a rough ocean with the goal to catch them."
- *Team 4 shows the Umbrella* and says, "This umbrella is *Relevant* when it's raining or sunny."
- *Team 5 shows the Female Runners* and says, "*Time-bound* means finishing at the right time. These women didn't finish their run before the rain started, so they were not time-bound."

What other ideas do you have for explaining the SMART acronym?

DEBRIEF QUESTIONS

Often, no debrief is required. Simply use this Photo Jolt to introduce or summarize other activities. This Photo Jolt can, however, act as a training tool. To get the most out of the activity, ask these questions:

- *Which part of the model was most difficult to explain? Why?*
- *Which part of the model was easiest to explain? Why?*
- *What paradoxes did we surface during our sharing?*
- *What surprised you in the responses?*
- *Was your team aligned in the responses?*
- *How did you resolve any debate?*
- *What was the most extreme response?*
- *Were your examples positive or negative? Why?*

If this is an opening activity, refer back to the findings as appropriate, "As Susan mentioned during our Photo Jolt, Time-bound means finishing at the right time. Why is that important?"

RESOURCES

- *Seven Sentence Stories Video*: Watch as Glenn explains "Seven Sentence Storytelling" at *http://YouTube.com/SMARTasHellVideo*
- *Seven Sentence Stories Template*: Download the Seven-Sentence Story template from *http://SMARTasHell.com*
- *Leadership Challenge*: Learn more about The Leadership Challenge at *http://LeadershipChallenge.com*

USE CASE

Creating Alignment

I'm a visual person; teased for the fact that I can't talk without drawing on a board - though, oddly, if you take away my marker, I keep talking. Anyway, the problem I have with words is that they give the impression of alignment.

You say, "Specific?"
They say, "Sure."
They say, "Shared Vision?"
You say, "I agree."
Ten minutes later, you're arguing about what the words mean.

I use Photo Jolts to pair a concrete image with a concept. Applications include The Leadership Challenge, DISC profiling, SMART goals, presentation skills training, innovation training, and much more.

When participants pair images with concepts, they create alignment and identify differences. Those differences can then be resolved, or at least acknowledged.

That's the power of Photo Jolts! activities.

- Glenn

50

LOOK, SEE, FEEL, EXPLORE, SHARE, CONNECT (LSFESC)

How deeply do you explore your situations?

We look, but we don't see. We see, but we don't feel. We feel, but we don't explore. We explore, but we don't share. We share, but we don't connect. What would happen if we took the time to look, see, feel, explore, share, and connect?

SYNOPSIS

Participants choose a photograph. They then deeply discuss the photograph with a partner.

PURPOSE

! *Clarity*: Provoke deep exploration of a situation or topic.

! *Creativity*: Apply metaphorical thinking to a situation or topic.

! *Conversation*: Share and connect deeply with colleagues.

TRAINING TOPICS

◆ *Solo*: How deeply can I explore this situation or topic?

◆ *One-on-One Coaching*: How deeply can we explore this situation or topic?

◆ *Customer Service:* Do I *Look, See, Feel, Explore, Share, Connect* with my customers? What would happen if I did?

◆ *Interviewing:* How can I learn more about someone through the *Look, See, Feel, Explore, Share, Connect* framework?

◆ *Problem Solving, Decision-making, Critical Thinking*: Have I considered this problem from different viewpoints?

◆ *Psychology:* How can I connect with others? How can I grow through this situation or topic?

◆ *Teamwork*: How can I work with others to explore this topic?

PARTICIPANTS

† *Minimum*: 2

† *Maximum*: any number

† *Best*: 2 to 32

† *Configurations*: Solo, Pairs, Triads, or Groups

TIME

🕐 *5 to 15 minutes*: Run 1 or 2 steps.

🕐 *15 to 30 minutes*: Drop 1 or 2 steps.

🕐 *30 to 60 minutes*: Run the full activity. Deep debrief.

PREPARATION

- Provide one deck of *Photo Jolts!* cards per 12 participants.
- <Optional> Provide one *LSFESC Worksheet* per participant.
- <Optional> Provide one *Emotional Vocabulary List (Table C)* per participant.
- <Optional> Provide one *Head-Heart-Guts-Groin-Bones Worksheet* per participant.

VIRTUAL FACILITATION OPTIONS (SEE PAGE 21)

✓ Remote Facilitation with Cards

FLOW

1. *Select a photograph.* Participants silently choose a photograph that resonates with them. This is their card for the entire exercise. Allow 1 to 2 minutes.
2. *Look.* Participants form groups of four or five and describe the scene literally to their teammates. Allow 3 minutes (30 seconds each).
3. *Define the situation or topic.* Introduce the participants to the situation or topic of the meeting, workshop, or event. (see *Table A*)
4. *See.* Participants describe how their image is a metaphor for the current situation or topic. Allow 3 minutes (30 seconds each).
5. *Feel.* Participants amplify their metaphor by describing how it makes them feel in their head, heart, gut, groin, and bones. Ask them to fill the 60 seconds with 'emotion' words. Teammates remain silent. Allow 5 minutes (60 seconds each).
6. *Explore.* Participants form triads. Participants then identify and share three to five mini-metaphors in their photo. These mini-

metaphors should support their feelings. Allow 6 minutes (2 min each).

7. *Share.* Participants form pairs. Using the same photo, share another time when they felt this way. When was it? What brought it about? How did the event turn out? How did they leverage the event? Partners should interview each other to share more information. Allow 6 minutes (3 min each).

8. *Connect.* Partners exchange photos. Participants then connect by discussing similarities in their stories. Partners explore how their photos might act as metaphors for each other's feelings. They then offer suggestions and support to each other. Allow 10 minutes (5 min each).

9. *<Optional> Share further.* Participants to share their partner's card with 4 other people in the room. Find common themes in the new group.

10. *Debrief.* This exercise is tied to the theme "We look, but we don't see. We see, but we don't feel. We feel, but we don't explore. We explore, but we don't share. We share, but we don't connect." Hand out the quote and debrief the activity.

VARIATIONS

- *Remove a Round*: Remove components of the activity to fit your time frame and intent. For example, you can ask participants to play "See, Explore, Connect" if you want to reduce the length of the exercise while encouraging connections.

- *6-Image-LSFESC:* Choose a different image for each step of the LSFESC activity.

PLAY SAMPLE

This sample uses *Photograph 1 - Skyscraper*. The topic for this discussion is 'Our Team'.

- *Look*: "This is a photograph of a modern skyscraper."
- *See*: "I believe that our team is hierarchical. Junior members don't get to contribute as much as senior members."
- *Feel*: "I feel like I have to wait 5 years before I can contribute. That's frustrating. Sometimes I get angry when my ideas aren't heard. I feel marginalized."
- *Explore*: "This photo is dark, which is how I feel at times. The windows are tiny, which represents my contribution. The building edges are sharp, like the rejection of my ideas."
- *Share*: "I was on a project team at college that felt this way. I didn't say anything. As a result, we didn't get the best ideas. We did sub-par work and got a poor grade. I don't want that to happen again."

- *Connect*: The partner replies, "I went through that in my previous company. I didn't like it, so I left. In retrospect, I wish I had talked with my teammates. My image shows two runners isolated from the drivers around them, but finding strength in each other's support. Do you have teammates that can support you?"

What other statements might you make?

DEBRIEF QUESTIONS

To get the most out of this Photo Jolt, show this quote and then ask the questions below:

We look, but we don't see.
We see, but we don't feel.
We feel, but we don't explore.
We explore, but we don't share.
We share, but we don't connect.

- *Which steps were difficult for you?*
- *What was gained through this exercise?*
- *What were common themes?*
- *What actions will you take out of this exercise?*

RESOURCES

- *LSFESC, Emotional Vocabulary, & Head-Heart-Gut-Groin-Bones Worksheets*: Download *Photo Jolts!* worksheets from *http://PhotoJolts.com*
- *LSFESC Quote/Slides*: Download the LSFESC Graphic from *http://PhotoJolts.com*

LSFESC WORKSHEET

Look: *What is the image?*

See: *What is the metaphor?*

Feel: *How do you feel?*

Explore: *Dig deeper. What are five 'mini-metaphors' in this image?*

Share: *When have you felt this way before?*

Connect: *What common experience does your partner have?*

HEAD-HEART-GUT-GROIN-BONES WORKSHEET

Head: *What are you feeling in your head? (Confusion? Stress? Etc.?)*

Heart: *What are you feeling in your heart? (Sadness? Joy? Etc.?)*

Gut: *What are you feeling in your gut? (Turmoil? Calm? Etc.?)*

Groin: *What are you feeling in your groin? (Pressure? Power? Etc.?)*

Bones: *What are you feeling in your bones? (Achy? Lightness? Etc.?)*

51
99-WORD PHOTO JOLT
(CONTRIBUTED BY BRIAN REMER)

What story does your picture tell?

Rod Stewart recorded the rock classic, "Every Picture Tells a Story," while Brian Remer, author of *Say It Quick*, suggests that we can tell powerful stories in just 99 words. What 99-word story does your picture tell?

SYNOPSIS

Participants choose a photograph. They then tell a 99-word story based on the image.

PURPOSE

! *Clarity*: Bring meaning to an ambiguous image.

! *Creativity*: Create the story behind an image.

! *Conversation*: Discuss the many alternative stories that can emerge from a single image.

TRAINING TOPICS

- *Solo*: Can I tell the story behind this image?

- *One-on-One Coaching*: Can you tell the story behind this image?

- *Icebreaker*: How can I explain our current situation in 99 words?

- *Communication*: Can I use words to make this image stronger?

- *Creativity*: How many stories can we create from one image?

- *Language / Vocabulary*: How do I best tell this story with exactly 99 words?

- *Any Training Topic*: Tie your stories to any training topic. See *Table A* for ideas.

PARTICIPANTS

✝ *Minimum*: 2

✝ *Maximum*: any number

✝ *Best*: 2 to 32

✝ *Configurations*: Solo, Pairs, Triads, or Groups

TIME

🕐 *5 to 15 minutes*: Run in pairs. No debrief.

🕐 *15 to 30 minutes*: Run pairs or triads. Short debrief.

🕐 *30 to 60 minutes*: Run in teams. Full debrief.

PREPARATION

- Provide one deck of *Photo Jolts!* cards per 12 participants.
- Provide paper and pens or pencils to the participants.
- <Optional> Provide *Say It Quick* by Brian Remer.

VIRTUAL FACILITATION OPTIONS (SEE PAGE 14)

- ✓ Image Sharing without Cards
- ✓ Video Sharing with Cards
- ✓ Audio Sharing with Cards
- ✓ Remote Facilitation with Cards

FLOW

1. *Select a photograph*. Participants silently choose a photograph that resonates with them. Allow 1 to 2 minutes.
2. *Write a story*. Participants write a 99-word story – yes, exactly 99 words – that lies behind their image. Allow 10 minutes.
3. *Share their story*. Participants share their story with their partner(s). Allow 2 minutes per participant.
4. *Debrief*. Debrief the activity.

VARIATIONS

- *99-Word Collage*: Form teams of four. Teams read a 99-word story from *Say It Quick*. The teams then create a 4-image collage that represents the story.
- *Let Me Show You*: Read a 99-word story from *Say It Quick*. Next, choose a random image and say, "Let me show you a picture from this story." Ask how it changes the interpretation of the story; what new insights it adds; and how one might alter the story or artwork to better reflect the concept.

- **99-Word Black Sheep**: Read a 99-word story from *Say it Quick*. Select two photos that represent the story and one that doesn't. Now, your partner (or another team) must guess which picture does not fit.

- **Transitions**: Read three 99-word stories. Insert two pictures as transitions between the three stories. These photographs should link the stories in a way that constructs a logical sequence and a larger story. Participants can choose the best sequence.

- **Narrative**: Your story must have a beginning, middle, and end with a challenge or complication. No informational essays are allowed.

PLAY SAMPLE

This sample uses *Photograph 5 - Umbrella*.

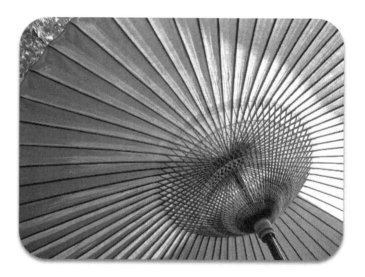

Red Paper Umbrella

Sometimes the best way to immerse in a new culture is also the simplest. You could learn about Japan by watching kabuki, learning nihongo, or practicing kendo. Or you could just sit under a red paper umbrella.

These umbrellas often provided me with refuge from the hot sun. I would relax, drink green tea, eat sweets, and gaze upward at a self-contained universe of craftsmanship.

Assembled from the simplest of materials - bamboo, thread, and paper - each umbrella creates a kaleidoscope of colors and patterns.

The umbrella is, like much in Japanese culture, simple, beautiful and practical.

What story would you write about this photo?

DEBRIEF QUESTIONS

To get the most out of this Photo Jolt, ask these questions:

- *What is the lesson in this story?*
- *Are there other lessons?*
- *What in this story applies to our situation or topic?*
- *Are there common themes in the group's stories?*
- *Are there contradictions in the group's stories?*
- *Which stories resonate with the group?*

RESOURCES

☞ *Say it Quick!* Find Brian Remer's *Say It Quick! 99-Word Stories About Leadership, Learning, and Life* at the *Thiagi.com* store.

☞ *Firefly.org* Learn more about Brian Remer and 99-Word Stories at *http://Firefly.org*

PART THREE

PHOTO
JOLTS!
RESOURCES

Modifying A Photo Jolt!

Photo Jolts! beg for modification. They want to be longer, shorter, easier, or more difficult, depending on the situation. Here are 27 approaches to modifying a Photo Jolt.

- *ADDITION*: Add elements to the Photo Jolt. Add a judge, a time limit, a camera, a worksheet, a prop, or sticky notes. Be creative.

- *ASSEMBLED*: Bring participant's individual work to pairs, triads, or groups and then assemble a collaborative product.

- *BUDDIES*: Stimulate new conversations. Each participant pairs up with a participant from a different team. Partners discuss the output and processes of their previous teams.

- *CHANGE THE NUMBERS / MORE OR LESS*: Change the number of cards to change the duration and/or difficulty of an activity.

- *COLLECTIVE CHOICE*: This modification requires pairs, triads, or groups to agree on a selection.

- *COMBINE WITH 'X'*: Combine any Photo Jolt with another Photo Jolt to increase the depth of the experience.

- *COMPLICATION*: Complicate a Photo Jolt with blindfolds, silence, or incomplete directions.

- *CONTINUOUS IMPROVEMENT*: Challenge the output from each team. Each team exchanges its output with the next team. They then work on improving the previous teams product.

- *DEBATE*: Stimulate more emotional and intellectual engagement. Each team persuades the other teams that their output is the best.

- *DUCK SEASON / RABBIT SEASON*: Turn the tables on participants by requiring them to change roles in the middle of an activity.

- *EVERYONE'S A COACH*: Empower attendees with expertise. Each team learns a different game. Teams are reorganized with members who know each game. They play all the games with the new expert explaining the flow.

- *GALLERY TOUR*: Get participants out of their chairs. Participants display their projects and then look at other's creations.

- *GAMIFICATION*: Make the Photo Jolt more game-like. Add a time element. Create a scoring system or a judge. Provide rewards and penalties.

- *IF I HAD MY DRUTHERS*: Help team members be heard. Ask each team member to explain what he or she would have done if left alone.

- *KEEP THE PROCESS; CHANGE THE CONTENT*: Challenge participants to improvise new activities. Participants must plagiarize the activity template and plug in different content.

- *KEEP THE CONTENT; CHANGE THE PROCESS*: Challenge participants to blow up old processes. Participants must use a different activity to achieve the same objective.

- *MICRO MANAGEMENT vs. EMPOWERMENT*: Provoke different team dynamics. Give some teams detailed instructions (organize into teams of five, choose team members you do not know, introduce yourself to the others…) while giving other teams vague explanations (form into teams of about five).

- *MIX AND MATCH*: Shake teams up. Members of each team count off "1, 2, 3, 4, 5." Participants then regroup with participants who share the same number … and continue the common task.

- *NO REDEEMING VALUE*: Let the inmates run the asylum. Participants must transform the activity into a party game without an instructional or organizational objective.

- *RANDOMIZE*: Add randomness to a Photo Jolt. Use dice, draw names out of a hat, or assign random numbers to mix up teams and other variables.

- *REINFORCE*: Reinforce an important theme. Look for situations, topics, lessons, values, or current events to highlight.

- *SELF-CONFESSION SESSION*: Stimulate constructive criticism. Each team member states one reason why the output or process sucks.

- *SEPARATION*: Create a virtual team environment. Place teams in separate rooms (or areas of a room) to complete a team project.

- *STAGGERED*: Break the Photo Jolt into sections and insert multiple debriefs. If a Photo Jolt has five steps, debrief each of the five steps.

- *SUBTRACTION*: Remove steps or materials from the Photo Jolt. Remove a worksheet, the instructions, or the time limit.

- *TABLE HOPPING*: Encourage sharing. Leave one host at each table with the final product. Others shift to the next table. The host explains the output. Others tweak it.

- *TEAM OR INDIVIDUAL*: Change the focus from team to individual or vice-versa. Run team activities for individuals. Run individual activities in teams.

Photo Jolts! Template

The question this Photo Jolt is designed to answer:

SYNOPSIS

Tells us - in one to three sentences - what happens in this activity.

PURPOSE (how does this activity increase clarity, creativity, or conversation?)

- *Clarity*: To
- *Creativity*: To
- *Conversation*: To

TRAINING TOPICS (what topics?)

- *Training Topic 1*:
- *Training Topic 2*:
- *Training Topic 3*:

PARTICIPANTS (how many?)

- *Minimum*:
- *Maximum*:
- *Best*:
- *Configurations*: Solo, Pairs, Triads, or Groups (circle all that apply)

TIME (how can this activity run in each timeframe?)

- *Less than 5 minutes*:
- *5 to 15 minutes*:
- *15 to 30 minutes*:
- *30 to 60 minutes*:

PREPARATION (what supplies or room set up is required?)

- One deck of *Photo Jolts!* cards per _____ participants.
- Worksheet?
- Other?

VIRTUAL FACILITATION OPTIONS (circle all that apply)

- ✓ *Image Sharing without Cards:*
- ✓ *Video Sharing with Cards:*
- ✓ *Audio Sharing with Cards:*
- ✓ *Remote Facilitation with Cards:*

FLOW

1.

2.

3.

4.

5.

6. Debrief.

VARIATIONS

- *Variation 1:*
- *Variation 2:*

PLAY SAMPLE

Here is a play sample for Photograph X.

- *Step one*:
- *Step two*:
- *Step three*:
- *Step four*:
- *Step five*:

DEBRIEF QUESTIONS

To get the most out of this Photo Jolt, discuss the following questions:

- *Q1*:
- *Q2*:
- *Q3*:

RESOURCES

- *Resource 1*:
- *Resource 2*:

MAKE PHOTO JOLTS STRONGER!

Photo Jolts! is a living, evolving project. We invite you to co-create and co-design *Photo Jolts!* in the following ways:

1. ***Distributed copy-editing.*** If you find typographical or conceptual errors in *Photo Jolts!* please let us know (*info@SMARTasHell.com*). We work with on-demand publishing technology that enables us to immediately incorporate your corrections and improvements.

2. ***Contribute new pieces of advice.*** Suggest additional pieces of advice based on your expertise and experience on different topics. We are not insistent about one particular way to achieve training goals in the interpersonal arena. So we welcome your unusual and innovative ideas as well as traditional and tried-and-true ones. We will collect and leverage your contributions in future editions.

3. ***Share additional resources.*** Let us know if you are aware of videos showing photo facilitation in action, image decks to add to our list, experiments or studies that support the use of photo facilitation, or useful books.

4. ***Share your use cases.*** Send us the stories you have from your use of *Photo Jolts!* Share big wins, horror stories, and small learning steps. If you're not sure how to tell your story, download the *Seven Sentence Story Template* from *SMARTasHell.com*.

5. ***Tweak our Photo Jolts!*** We do not expect an experienced facilitator like you to conscientiously follow our instructions for conducting these activities. Please let us know if you have come up with variations or improvements of the current set of activities. We will post your ideas on our website and incorporate them in the next version of *Photo Jolts!*

6. *Create new activities.* Contribute your new games or ideas for the next edition of *Photo Jolts!* and get a free copy of the book if your suggestion makes the final cut. You can complete the *Photo Jolts!* Template, although this step is not required.

7. *Provide a review.* We love to get your unbiased reviews of our books on Amazon, BarnesandNoble.com, or Goodreads. Our favorite reviews simply state, "I had a problem. I used Photo Jolt! #XX. It helped my problem."

8. *Request additional features.* If there are general additions - chapters, graphics, tools, worksheets, videos - that you would like to see incorporated in future editions, let us know.

9. *Suggest additional decks.* We currently offer *Photo Jolts!, Animal Jolts!, People Jolts!, Poker Jolts!,* and *Photo Provocations.* We are continuously researching additional topics for *Photo Jolts!* decks. Let us know what topics or subjects will make it easier for you to facilitate your *Photo Jolts!* sessions.

10. *Visit our web sites.* We will post our updates, new games, variations, and field notes at *SMARTasHell.com* and *Thiagi.com.* You can post your ideas, comments, and suggestions there.

And remember, your easiest one-stop contact is *info@SMARTasHell.com*

GET MORE PHOTO JOLTS!

We've provided multiple ways to continue your *Photo Jolts!* experience:

- *Websites*: *SMARTasHell.com* and *Thiagi.com*
- *Email*: *info@SMARTasHell.com* or *thiagi@thiagi.com*
- *YouTube:* *YouTube.com/SMARTasHellVideo*
- *Twitter*: *twitter.com/SMARTasHell* and *twitter.com/Thiagi*
- *LinkedIn:* In the SMART as Hell LinkedIn group
- *Pinterest*: *pinterest.com/SMARTasHell/PhotoJolts/*
- *Instagram*: *instagram.com/glenn_hughes*
- *Amazon Author Page*: *amazon.com/author/ghughes*
- *Goodreads*: *goodreads.com/GlennHughes*
- *Photo Jolts! Workshops & Certification*: Our workshops are conducted in-person or virtually.
- *Photo Jolts! Image Store*: *hues.smugmug.com*
- *Photo Jolts! Style*: Get *Photo Jolts!* shirts, mugs, mouse pads and more at *zazzle.com/smartashell*
- *Photo Jolts! Books*: Buy *Photo Jolts!* in print (at *amazon.com*, *PhotoJolts.com*, and *Thiagi.com*), or e-book (at *amazon.com*, *barnesandnoble.com*, and *iTunes*). Email us for quantity discounts or bundles.
- *Photo Jolts! card decks*. *Photo Jolts!*, *Animal Jolts!*, *People Jolts!*, *Food Jolts!*, *Nature Jolts!*, *Poker Jolts! ArchiJolts!* and *Photo Provocations*. Want to customize *Photo Jolts!* decks with your logo for offsites, conferences, or customer gifts? Curious about quantity pricing? Email *info@SMARTasHell.com*

Image Card Sources

The companies below sell a wide range of image sets. Don't hesitate to mix and match images to build your perfect deck.

- **Photo Jolts!** (*www.PhotoJolts.com*)
- **Visual Explorer** (*www.ccl.org*)
- **VisualsSpeak** (*www.visualsspeak.com*)
- **Picture This** (*www.InnovativeResources.org*)
- **PicTour Imagine** (*www.SherlockCreativeThinking.com*)
- **Postcard Processing Kit** (*store.Training-Wheels.com*)
- **Curiosity Box** (*www.CuriousMindsco.com.au*)
- **Points of You** (*www.CoachingToysStore.com*)
- **Pick a Postcard** (*www.CoachingToysStore.com*)
- **Oh Cards** (*www.oh-cards.com*)
- **ColorCards** (*www.TherapeuticResources.com*)

TABLE A: PHOTO JOLTS! TOPICS

"Pick a photo that's a metaphor for _____ "

- Leadership
- Management
- Teamwork
- Culture
- Diversity
- Creativity
- Marketing
- Branding
- Sales
- Advertising
- Field Service
- Customer Service
- Finance
- Technical Support
- Government
- Work
- Development
- Goals
- Training
- College
- Travel
- Conflict
- Communication
- Ethics
- Human Resources
- IT
- Presentations
- Logistics
- Strategy
- Time Management
- Art
- Design
- Interviewing
- Politics
- Religion

- The Economic Situation
- Travel
- Marriage
- Your Values
- Your First 90 Days
- Your Leadership Style
- Your Personality
- Your Team
- Your Culture
- Your Hidden Side
- Your Company
- Your Product
- Your Challenge
- Your Opportunity
- Your Relationship with __
- Your Financial Situation
- Your Work/Life Balance
- Your Job
- Your Development
- Your Goals
- A Development Area
- Your Education
- Your Industry
- Your Competition
- Your Customer
- Your Vendor
- Your Childhood
- Your Parents
- Your Family
- Your Dreams
- Your Greatest Success
- Your Greatest Failure
- Your Strength(s)
- Your Weakness(es)

TABLE B: DUALITIES

"Pick two photos that are metaphors for _____"

- Work vs. Play
- Light vs. Dark
- Alive vs. Dead
- Ally vs. Enemy
- East vs. West
- False vs. True
- Authentic vs. Fake
- Local vs. Global
- Peace vs. War
- Fast vs. Slow
- Child vs. Adult
- Male vs. Female
- Trust vs. Distrust
- Public vs. Private
- Past vs. Present
- Past vs. Future
- Yin vs. Yang
- Give vs. Take
- Life vs. Death
- Left vs. Right
- Love vs. Hate
- Art vs. Science
- 'Us' vs. 'Them'
- Job vs. Family
- Hero vs. Villain
- Rich vs. Poor
- Cost vs. Quality
- Reap vs. Sow
- Good vs. Bad
- Young vs. Old
- Pure vs. Impure
- Smart vs. Dumb
- Present vs. Future
- Guilty vs. Innocent
- Inside vs. Outside

- Master vs. Servant
- Nature vs. Nurture
- Intrinsic vs. Extrinsic
- Safe vs. Dangerous
- Art vs. Commerce
- Leading vs. Following
- Teamwork vs. Individual
- Creative vs. Stagnant
- Strategy vs. Tactics
- Ethical vs. Unethical
- Conflict vs. Consensus
- Strength vs. Weakness
- Dream vs. Nightmare
- Liberal vs. Conservative
- Finished vs. Unfinished
- Horizontal vs. Vertical
- Best vs. Worst Days
- Best vs. Worst Boss
- Best vs. Worst Job
- Best vs. Worst Customer
- Best vs. Worst Service
- Best vs. Worst Design
- Best vs. Worst Decision
- Best vs. Worst Marketing
- Best vs. Worst Sales
- Book-smart vs. Street-smart
- Inspires vs. Frightens you
- Evolutionary vs. Revolutionary
- Leadership vs. Management
- Republican vs. Democrat
- Junior vs. Senior

TABLE C: EMOTIONAL VOCABULARY

"I feel..."

- Abandoned
- Affection
- Aggravated
- Aggressive
- Agitated
- Alert
- Amazed
- Anger
- Annoyed
- Appreciative
- Apprehensive
- Aroused
- Ashamed
- Betrayed
- Bewildered
- Bitter
- Bored
- Calm
- Cautious
- Cheerful
- Cocky
- Cold
- Concerned
- Confident
- Confused
- Content
- Courageous
- Curious
- Delighted
- Dejected
- Determined

- Devastated
- Disgust
- Down
- Ecstatic
- Embarrassed
- Empty
- Enraged
- Excited
- Exhausted
- Fascinated
- Fear
- Foolish
- Frustrated
- Gloomy
- Goofy
- Grateful
- Greedy
- Grouchy
- Guilty
- Happy
- Hate
- Hurt
- Insecure
- Inspired
- Interested
- Intimidated
- Irritated
- Jealousy
- Joy
- Lazy
- Liberated

- Lonely
- Love
- Lust
- Mean
- Mellow
- Needy
- Nervous
- Offended
- Optimistic
- Overwhelmed
- Peaceful
- Pessimistic
- Playful
- Proud
- Remorse
- Sadness
- Scared
- Shame
- Shocked
- Shy
- Sorry
- Submissive
- Surprised
- Thrilled
- Troubled
- Unhappy
- Upset
- Warm
- Worried

TABLE D: TOPICS CROSS-REFERENCE

Anywhere Jolts

- 02 A Thousand Words
- 03 Another Thousand Words
- 07 Emotional Rescue
- 08 User Experience
- 09 Empathy
- 12 Black Sheep
- 15 Visual Memory
- 18 Naturalist
- 19 Soundtrack
- 20 Textures
- 21 Deeper
- 24 Sunny Monkey
- 25 Eyes Wide Open
- 26 Book by its Cover
- 27 Bizarro World
- 29 Postcards from…
- 36 Optimist & Pessimist
- 40 And Then…
- 46 An Open and Closed Case
- 48 Lessons from…

Art

- 42 Police Artist
- 43 White Space
- 44 Redraw

Business

- 18 Naturalist
- 28 Present
- 32 Risk Assessment
- 33 Build an Organization
- 36 Optimist & Pessimist
- 42 Police Artist

Coaching

All of the Photo Jolts are applicable to one-on-one coaching situations

Communication

- 01 Photo Jolted!
- 06 Perspectives
- 07 Emotional Rescue
- 08 User Experience
- 10 Silent Selection
- 13 Categories
- 14 Lotus Blossom
- 19 Soundtrack
- 20 Textures
- 21 Deeper
- 24 Sunny Monkey
- 26 Book by its Cover
- 29 Postcards from…
- 30 Captions
- 33 Build an Organization
- 37 Classified Ad
- 38 Kipling's Questions
- 39 Sequencing
- 40 And Then…
- 42 Police Artist
- 44 Redraw
- 45 Half-life
- 47 Recipe for Success
- 51 99-Word Photo Jolt

Creativity

- 02 A Thousand Words
- 03 Another Thousand Words
- 08 User Experience
- 12 Black Sheep
- 19 Soundtrack
- 20 Textures
- 24 Sunny Monkey
- 25 Creativity
- 26 Book by its Cover
- 29 Postcards from…
- 30 Captions
- 31 Quarters
- 32 Risk Assessment
- 33 Build an Organization
- 34 Time Machine
- 35 Stages
- 36 Optimist & Pessimist
- 40 And Then…
- 41 Problem / Solution
- 43 White Space
- 45 Half-life
- 47 Recipe for Success
- 48 Lessons from…
- 51 99-Word Photo Jolt

Culture, Diversity, Perception

- 01 Photo Jolted!
- 06 Perspectives
- 07 Emotional Rescue
- 08 User Experience
- 11 Teams
- 12 Black Sheep
- 17 Ethnographer
- 18 Naturalist
- 19 Soundtrack
- 20 Textures
- 22 Notice
- 29 Postcards from…
- 35 Stages

- 36 Optimist & Pessimist

Customer Service

- 06 Perspectives
- 09 Empathy
- 12 Black Sheep
- 28 Present
- 31 Quarters
- 43 White Space
- 51 Look, See, Feel, Explore, Share, Connect

Design

- 08 User Experience
- 14 Lotus Blossom
- 19 Soundtrack
- 20 Textures
- 21 Deeper
- 22 Notice
- 26 Book by its Cover
- 30 Captions
- 31 Quarters
- 34 Time Machine
- 44 Redraw
- 45 Half-life
- 48 Lessons from…

Icebreaker

- 01 Photo Jolted!
- 02 A Thousand Words
- 03 Another Thousand Words
- 12 Black Sheep
- 43 White Space
- 51 99-Word Photo Jolt

Interviewing

- 07 Emotional Rescue
- 12 Black Sheep
- 38 Kipling's Questions
- 42 Police Artist
- 46 An Open and Closed Case
- 51 Look, See, Feel, Explore, Share, Connect

Language / Vocabulary

- 21 Deeper
- 24 Sunny Monkey
- 37 Classified Ad
- 51 99-Word Photo Jolt

Leadership

- 04 A Christmas Carol
- 05 Building the Bridge
- 10 Silent Selection
- 32 Risk Assessment
- 34 Time Machine
- 38 Kipling's Questions
- 43 White Space
- 46 An Open and Closed Case
- 47 Recipe for Success

Observation Skills

- 15 Visual Memory
- 16 Insert and Remove
- 17 Ethnographer
- 18 Naturalist
- 19 Soundtrack
- 20 Textures
- 21 Deeper
- 22 Notice
- 23 Clues
- 25 Creativity
- 35 Stages
- 41 Problem / Solution

Philosophy

- 03 Another Thousand Words
- 27 Bizarro World
- 36 Optimist & Pessimist

Problem Solving

- 10 Silent Selection
- 11 Teams
- 12 Black Sheep
- 13 Categories
- 14 Lotus Blossom
- 15 Visual Memory
- 16 Insert and Remove
- 17 Ethnographer
- 18 Naturalist
- 21 Deeper
- 31 Quarters
- 32 Risk Assessment
- 33 Build an Organization
- 34 Time Machine
- 35 Stages
- 37 Classified Ad
- 38 Kipling's Questions
- 41 Problem / Solution
- 42 Police Artist
- 43 White Space
- 44 Redraw
- 46 An Open and Closed Case
- 47 Recipe for Success
- 48 Lessons From…
- 51 Look, See, Feel, Explore, Share, Connect

Psychology

- 01 Photo Jolted!
- 07 Emotional Rescue
- 09 Empathy
- 10 Silent Selection

Psychology cont'd

- 11 Teams
- 15 Visual Memory
- 16 Insert and Remove
- 25 Creativity
- 27 Bizarro World
- 28 Present
- 37 Classified Ad
- 51 Look, See, Feel, Explore, Share, Connect

Recommended for Kids

- 01 Photo Jolted!
- 07 Emotional Rescue
- 09 Empathy
- 12 Black Sheep
- 18 Naturalist
- 19 Soundtrack
- 25 Eyes Wide Open
- 26 Book by its Cover
- 29 Captions
- 39 Sequencing
- 40 And Then
- 41 Police Artist
- 43 White Space
- 44 Redraw
- 51 99-Word Photo Jolt

Sales and Marketing

- 08 User Experience
- 09 Empathy
- 21 Deeper
- 23 Clues
- 24 Sunny Monkey
- 26 Book by its Cover
- 27 Bizarro World
- 28 Present
- 29 Postcards from…
- 30 Captions
- 37 Classified Ad
- 39 Sequencing

- 46 An Open and Closed Case

Sciences

- 13 Categories
- 18 Naturalist

Teamwork

- 04 A Christmas Carol
- 06 Perspectives
- 10 Silent Selection
- 11 Teams
- 13 Categories
- 15 Visual Memory
- 16 Insert and Remove
- 19 Soundtrack
- 20 Textures
- 39 Sequencing
- 40 And Then…
- 45 Half-life
- 51 Look, See, Feel, Explore, Share, Connect

Training

- 02 A Thousand Words
- 03 Another Thousand Words
- 09 Empathy
- 18 Naturalist
- 23 Clues
- 24 Sunny Monkey
- 29 Postcards from…
- 39 Sequencing
- 45 Half-life
- 47 Recipe for Success
- 48 Lessons from…
- 49 Training Photos
- 51 99-Word Photo Jolt

TABLE E: IMAGE SCORECARD

Are your images appropriate for a *Photo Jolts!* activity? Assess your images with this scorecard. A strong image set should achieve a score of nine points or higher. For more information, see pages 6-7.

	No 0 Points	Yes 1 Point	Exceeding 2 Points
Are the images High Resolution?	Unclear. Torn. Pixilated. Folded. Dirty.	Clear. Easy to view. Minimal pixilation, dirt, tears.	Crystalline. High Definition. No folds, dirt, or tears.
Are the images High Impact?	Not compelling. Not engaging. Participants set them aside easily.	Interesting. Attract the attention of busy, distracted participants.	Compelling. Participants want to keep images after the session.
Are the images Immersive?	One-dimensional. Can be explored completely in five to ten seconds.	Two-dimensional. Requires ten or more seconds to explore.	Multi-dimensional. Participants return to the image again and again.
Are the images Ambiguous?	Overly negative or positive. Most participants would create similar metaphor.	Will be interpreted both positively and negatively. Creates a range of metaphors.	Creates a dramatic range of metaphors, even from a single participant.
Are the images Global & Varied?	No range of subjects, colors, emotional content, countries, or cultures.	Limited range of image content. Images are overly familiar.	Wide range of image content. Strong mix of familiar and unfamiliar images.
Are the images Sturdy?	Flimsy. Unsubstantial. Tears easily.	Robust. Substantial. Can be reused.	Laminated or embossed. Holds up well to extended reuse.

TABLE F: ACTIVITY SCORECARD

Was your *Photo Jolts!* activity successful? Assess the activity with this scorecard. A score of eight points or higher is strong; twelve or more is excellent. Use this sheet to identify areas of success and areas for improvement.

	No 0 Points	Yes 1 Point	Exceeding 2 Points
Was your goal achieved?	Goal was not achieved.	Goal was achieved.	Goal was exceeded.
Was the purpose clear and appropriate?	No purpose was identified.	Purpose was appropriate, but not clear to participants.	Purpose was appropriate and clear to participants.
Was time well-managed?	Too short or too long for goal/purpose.	Too short or too long for time slot.	Activity was appropriate for time slot and purpose.
Were you prepared?	Not prepared.	Prepared for activity.	Prepared for activity and changes.
Did you follow the activity flow?	No. Failed to follow the scripted Flow.	Yes. Followed scripted Flow.	Yes, after consciously altering the scripted Flow.
Was the debrief effective?	No debrief was held.	The debrief provided clarity, but no insights.	The debrief provided deep insights.
Were participants engaged?	No. They were bored or distracted.	Yes. Most participated as asked.	Totally! They didn't want to end the activity.
Was photo facilitation the best tool?	No. Not for this purpose	Maybe. Other tools could also have achieved this result.	Yes. No other tool could have achieved this result.

ABOUT THE AUTHORS

Glenn Hughes, an award-winning photographer and facilitator, is Director of Global Learning at KLA-Tencor, a leading provider of process control and yield management solutions. KLA-Tencor's learning organization was recognized in 2008 as a charter member of TRAINING Magazine's *"Training Top 10 Hall of Fame"* after placing in the world's Top 10 Training Organizations for 5 consecutive years.

Glenn is also the founder of SMART as Hell, a company that helps individuals and organizations change their world one goal at a time. SMART as Hell develops best practices in goal writing and achievement – including the groundbreaking *SMARTometer*, a tool for measuring the effectiveness of goals.

Glenn lived in Asia for more than 10 years, working with many of the world's largest electronics companies while managing multi-million dollar operations in China, Singapore, and Japan. He holds a Master's Degree in Adult Education and Training and a Bachelor's Degree in Electronics Engineering Technology. Glenn's instructional design credits include:

- Duarte Design's *slide:ology*
- Group Harmonics' *Make Work Great*
- Power Speaking's *Speaking Up*
- Robert Thompson's *The Offsite: A Leadership Simulation*

In 2013, Glenn received two 2013 Facilitation Impact Awards from the International Association of Facilitators, recognizing the world-class results that he and his clients have achieved. He is a frequent speaker at international conferences such as the American Society for Training and Development, the International Society for Performance Improvement, Lakewood's TRAINING Conferences, and the International Association of Facilitators.

Dr. Sivasailam 'Thiagi' Thiagarajan is the Resident Mad Scientist at The Thiagi Group, an organization with the mission of helping people improve their performance effectively and enjoyably. Thiagi's long-term clients include AT&T, Arthur Andersen, Bank of Montreal, Cadence Design Systems, Chevron, IBM, Intel, Intelsat, United Airlines, and Liberty Mutual.

Thiagi has published 40 books, 120 games and simulations, and more than 200 articles. His credits include:

- *Jolts!*
- *More Jolts!*
- *Thiagi's 100 Favorite Games*
- *Design Your Own Games and Activities*
- *Framegames*
- *Simulation Games*
- *Thiagi's Interactive Lectures*

Thiagi has made hundreds of presentations and keynote speeches at professional conferences, including the International Society for Performance Improvement (ISPI), Lakewood's TRAINING Conferences, and the annual conferences of American Society for Training and Development (ASTD) and North American Simulation and Gaming Association (NASAGA).

Thiagi has been the president of the North American Simulation and Gaming Associating (NASAGA), International Society for Performance Improvement (ISPI), and Association for Special Education Technology (ASET). He has received 17 different awards and Presidential Citations from ISPI, including the society's highest award, Honorary Life Member. He also received an Honorary Life Member award from NASAGA as well as its highest award, Ifill-Raynolds Award.

Internationally recognized as an expert in multinational collaboration and active learning in organizations, Thiagi has lived in three different countries and has consulted in 21 others.

CONTACT US:

Contact Glenn Hughes at:

- SMARTasHell.com
- info@SMARTasHell.com

Contact Thiagi at:

- Thiagi.com

Links for Photo Jolts!

http://SMARTasHell.com/blog/pjresources